BAD ASS

COOKBOOK

Some of the products listed in this publication may be in limited distribution.

Artwork on interior pages © Shutterstock.com

Pictured on the front cover: Chicken Fajita Nachos (*page 20*).

Pictured on the back cover (*left to right*): Spicy Pork Po' Boys (*page 72*), Onion Ring Stack (*page 138*), and Ice Cream Pizza Treat (*page 174*).

ISBN: 978-1-64030-632-5

Manufactured in China.

8 7 6 5 4 3 2 1

Microwave Cooking: Microwave ovens vary in wattage. Use the cooking times as guidelines and check for doneness before adding more time.

PRETZEL STICKS WITH BEER-CHEESE DIP *(page 6)*   PUB-STYLE FISH & CHIPS *(page 96)*   CHOCOLATE CAKE MILKSHAKE *(page 172)*

TABLE OF CONTENTS

HARD CORE STARTERS

BEEF AND BEER SLIDERS

MAKES 12 SLIDERS

- 6 tablespoons ketchup
- 2 tablespoons mayonnaise
- 2 teaspoons Dijon mustard
- 1½ pounds ground beef
- ½ cup beer
- 1 teaspoon salt
- ½ teaspoon garlic powder
- ½ teaspoon onion powder
- ½ teaspoon ground cumin
- ½ teaspoon dried oregano
- ¼ teaspoon black pepper
- 3 slices sharp Cheddar cheese, cut into 4 pieces
- 12 slider buns or potato dinner rolls
- 12 baby lettuce leaves
- 12 plum tomato slices

1 Combine ketchup, mayonnaise and mustard in small bowl; reserve.

2 Combine beef, beer, salt, garlic powder, onion powder, cumin, oregano and pepper in medium bowl. Shape mixture into 12 (¼-inch-thick) patties.

3 Prepare grill for direct cooking over medium-high heat. Spray grid with nonstick cooking spray. Grill patties 2 minutes. Turn; top each with 1 piece cheese. Grill 2 minutes or until cheese is melted and patties are cooked through. Remove to large plate; keep warm.

4 Serve sliders on rolls with ketchup mixture, lettuce and tomato.

PRETZEL STICKS WITH BEER-CHEESE DIP

MAKES 6 TO 8 SERVINGS (2 CUPS DIP)

PRETZELS

- 1⅔ cups warm water (110° to 115°F)
- 1 package (¼ ounce) active dry yeast
- 2 teaspoons sugar
- 1 teaspoon table salt
- 4½ cups all-purpose flour, plus additional for work surface
- 2 tablespoons butter, softened
- 2 tablespoons vegetable oil
- 12 cups water
- ½ cup baking soda
- Kosher salt or pretzel salt and sesame seeds

HONEY-MUSTARD DIP

- ⅓ cup sour cream
- ¼ cup Dijon mustard
- 3 tablespoons honey

BEER-CHEESE DIP

- 2 tablespoons butter
- 1 clove garlic, minced
- 2 tablespoons all-purpose flour
- 1 tablespoon Dijon mustard
- 1 teaspoon Worcestershire sauce
- 1 cup Belgian white ale
- 2 cups (8 ounces) shredded white Cheddar cheese
- 1 cup (4 ounces) shredded Monterey Jack cheese
- Black pepper (optional)

1 Combine 1⅔ cups warm water, yeast, sugar and 1 teaspoon salt in large bowl of electric stand mixer; stir to dissolve yeast. Let stand 5 minutes or until bubbly. Add 4½ cups flour and softened butter; beat at low speed until combined, scraping side of bowl occasionally. Replace paddle attachment with dough hook; knead at medium-low speed 5 minutes.

2 Place dough in large greased bowl; turn to coat top. Cover and let rise in warm place 1 hour or until doubled in size.

3 For mustard dip, combine sour cream, ¼ cup mustard and honey in small bowl; mix well. Refrigerate until ready to use.

4 Preheat oven to 450°F. Brush 1 tablespoon oil over each of 2 large baking sheets. Bring 12 cups water to a boil in large saucepan or Dutch oven.

5 Punch down dough; turn out onto floured work surface. Flatten and stretch dough into 14 equal pieces. Roll each piece into 12-inch-long rope. Cut each rope in half.

6

6 Carefully stir baking soda into boiling water. Working in batches, drop dough pieces into boiling water; cook 30 seconds. Remove to prepared baking sheets with slotted spoon. Make 3 to 4 slashes in each pretzel stick with sharp knife. Sprinkle with kosher salt and sesame seeds.

7 Bake 14 to 15 minutes or until dark golden brown, rotating baking sheets halfway through baking time. Cool slightly on wire rack.

8 Meanwhile for cheese dip, melt 2 tablespoons butter in medium saucepan over medium heat. Add garlic; cook and stir 1 minute. Whisk in 2 tablespoons flour until well blended; cook 1 minute. Whisk in 1 tablespoon mustard and Worcestershire sauce. Slowly whisk in ale in thin steady stream. Cook 1 minute or until slightly thickened. Add cheeses by ¼ cupfuls, stirring until cheeses are melted before adding next addition. Transfer to serving bowl; sprinkle with pepper, if desired. Serve pretzels warm with dips.

TEX-MEX NACHOS

MAKES 4 TO 6 SERVINGS

1 tablespoon
vegetable oil

8 ounces ground beef

½ cup chopped onion

2 cloves garlic, minced

2 teaspoons chili
powder

1 teaspoon ground
cumin

½ teaspoon salt

½ teaspoon dried
oregano

1 can (about
15 ounces) kidney
beans, rinsed and
drained

½ cup corn

½ cup sour cream,
divided

2 tablespoons
mayonnaise

1 tablespoon lime
juice

¼ to ½ teaspoon
chipotle chili
powder

½ bag tortilla chips

½ (15-ounce) jar
Cheddar cheese
dip, warmed

½ cup pico de gallo

¼ cup guacamole

1 cup shredded iceberg
lettuce

2 jalapeño peppers,*
thinly sliced into rings

*Jalapeño peppers can sting
and irritate the skin, so wear
rubber gloves when handling
peppers and do not touch
your eyes.*

1 Heat oil in large skillet over medium-high heat. Add beef, onion and garlic; cook and stir 6 minutes or until beef is no longer pink. Add chili powder, cumin, salt and oregano; cook and stir 1 minute. Add beans and corn; reduce heat to medium-low and cook 3 minutes or until heated through.

2 For chipotle sauce, combine ¼ cup sour cream, mayonnaise, lime juice and chipotle chili powder in small bowl; mix well. Place in small plastic squeeze bottle.

3 Spread tortilla chips on platter or large plate. Top with beef mixture; drizzle with cheese dip. Top with pico de gallo, guacamole, remaining ¼ cup sour cream, lettuce and jalapeño peppers. Squeeze chipotle sauce over nachos. Serve immediately.

BEER-BRAISED MEATBALLS

MAKES 20 MEATBALLS

- 1 pound ground beef
- ½ cup seasoned dry bread crumbs
- ½ cup grated Parmesan cheese
- 2 eggs, lightly beaten
- ⅓ cup finely chopped onion
- 2 cloves garlic, minced
- ½ teaspoon black pepper
- ¼ teaspoon salt
- 1 bottle (12 ounces) light-colored beer, such as lager
- 1½ cups tomato sauce
- 1 cup ketchup
- 2 tablespoons tomato paste
- ½ cup packed brown sugar

1 Preheat oven to 400°F. Line broiler pan with foil; spray rack with nonstick cooking spray.

2 Combine beef, bread crumbs, cheese, eggs, onion, garlic, pepper and salt in large bowl; stir to blend. Shape mixture into 1-inch balls. Place meatballs on prepared rack. Bake 10 minutes or until browned.

3 Bring beer, tomato sauce, ketchup, tomato paste and brown sugar to a boil in Dutch oven. Add meatballs and reduce heat to medium-low. Cover; simmer 20 to 30 minutes or until meatballs are cooked through, stirring occasionally.

SPICY BBQ PARTY FRANKS ➲
MAKES 6 TO 8 SERVINGS

1 tablespoon butter

1 package (1 pound) cocktail franks

⅓ cup cola beverage

⅓ cup ketchup

2 tablespoons hot pepper sauce

2 tablespoons packed dark brown sugar

1 tablespoon cider vinegar

1 Melt butter in medium skillet over medium heat. Pierce cocktail franks with fork. Add franks to skillet; cook until slightly browned.

2 Stir in cola, ketchup, hot pepper sauce, brown sugar and vinegar. Reduce heat to low; cook until sauce is reduced to sticky glaze.

BACON-WRAPPED BBQ CHICKEN
MAKES 4 SERVINGS

8 chicken tenders (about 1 pound)

½ teaspoon paprika or ground cumin (optional)

8 slices bacon

½ cup barbecue sauce

1 Preheat broiler. Line broiler pan with foil.

2 Sprinkle chicken tenders with paprika, if desired. Wrap each chicken tender with 1 slice of bacon in spiral pattern; place on prepared pan.

3 Broil chicken 4 minutes. Turn and broil 2 minutes. Brush with ¼ cup barbecue sauce; broil 2 minutes. Turn and brush with remaining ¼ cup barbecue sauce; broil 2 minutes or until chicken is no longer pink in center.

SPICY KOREAN CHICKEN WINGS

MAKES 6 TO 8 SERVINGS

2 tablespoons peanut oil, plus additional for frying

2 tablespoons grated fresh ginger

½ cup reduced-sodium soy sauce

¼ cup cider vinegar

¼ cup honey

¼ cup chili garlic sauce

2 tablespoons orange juice

1 tablespoon dark sesame oil

18 chicken wings or drummettes

Sesame seeds (optional)

1 Heat 2 tablespoons peanut oil in medium skillet over medium-high heat. Add ginger; cook and stir 1 minute. Add soy sauce, vinegar, honey, chili garlic sauce, orange juice and sesame oil; cook and stir 2 minutes.

2 Heat 2 inches of peanut oil in large heavy saucepan over medium-high heat to 350° to 375°F; adjust heat to maintain temperature.

3 Rinse wings under cold water; pat dry with paper towels. Remove and discard wing tips.

4 Add wings to oil and cook 8 to 10 minutes or until crispy and browned and chicken is cooked through. Remove to paper towel-lined plate.

5 Add wings to sauce; toss to coat. Sprinkle with sesame seeds, if desired.

HOT CHEESE-CHIPOTLE DIP

MAKES 8 SERVINGS (3 CUPS DIP)

- 2 tablespoons unsalted butter
- 1 onion, chopped
- ½ red bell pepper, finely chopped
- 1 clove garlic, minced
- 2 tablespoons all-purpose flour
- 1 can (about 14 ounces) diced tomatoes, 2 tablespoons juice reserved
- 1 cup lager or pilsner beer, preferably Mexican
- 1 canned chipotle pepper in adobo sauce, minced, plus 1 teaspoon adobo sauce
- 4 cups (16 ounces) shredded Mexican-style cheese blend
  Chopped fresh cilantro (optional)
  Tortilla chips

1 Melt butter in medium saucepan over medium heat. Add onion, bell pepper and garlic; cook and stir 5 minutes or until tender. Add flour; stir until well blended. Stir in tomatoes and reserved juice, lager, chipotle pepper and adobo sauce; bring to a boil. Reduce heat to low; simmer 5 minutes or until thickened.

2 Remove from heat. Stir in cheese blend, 1 cup at a time, until each addition is melted. If necessary, return to very low heat and stir just until melted. Sprinkle with cilantro, if desired. Serve warm with tortilla chips.

NOTE

Don't overcook the cheese, or this dip will become gritty.

TIP: For a zestier flavor, add more adobo sauce from the canned chipotle.

SPICY ALE SHRIMP
MAKES 15 TO 20 SHRIMP

Dipping Sauce
(recipe follows)

3 bottles (12 ounces
   each) pilsner beer,
   divided

1 tablespoon seafood
   boil seasoning
   blend

1 teaspoon mustard
   seeds

1 teaspoon red pepper
   flakes

2 lemons, quartered
   and divided

1 pound large raw
   shrimp, peeled
   and deveined
   (with tails on)

1 Prepare Dipping Sauce; set aside. Pour 1 bottle of beer into large bowl half-filled with ice; set aside.

2 Fill large saucepan half full with water. Add remaining 2 bottles of beer, seafood seasoning, mustard seeds and red pepper flakes. Squeeze 4 lemon quarters into saucepan and add lemon quarters. Bring to a boil over medium-high heat.

3 Add shrimp to saucepan; cover and remove from heat. Let stand 3 minutes or until shrimp are pink and opaque. Drain shrimp; transfer to bowl of chilled beer and ice. Cool. Remove shrimp from bowl; arrange on platter. Serve with Dipping Sauce and remaining lemon quarters.

DIPPING SAUCE
MAKES ABOUT 1 CUP SAUCE

1 cup ketchup

1 tablespoon
   chili-garlic paste

1 tablespoon prepared
   horseradish

   Juice of 1 lime

   Hot pepper sauce

Combine ketchup, chili-garlic paste, horseradish and lime juice in small bowl. Add hot pepper sauce to taste; mix well. Cover and refrigerate 1 hour.

CHICKEN FAJITA NACHOS
MAKES 4 SERVINGS

2 tablespoons vegetable oil, divided

2 red bell peppers, cut into thin strips

1 large onion, halved and thinly sliced

2 tablespoons fajita seasoning mix (from 1¼-ounce package), divided

2 tablespoons water, divided

12 ounces boneless skinless chicken breast, cut into 2×1-inch strips

4 cups tortilla chips (about 30 chips)

½ cup (2 ounces) shredded Cheddar cheese

½ cup (2 ounces) shredded Monterey Jack cheese

1 jalapeño pepper,* seeded and thinly sliced

1 cup shredded lettuce

½ cup salsa, plus additional for serving

Sour cream and guacamole (optional)

Jalapeño peppers can sting and irritate the skin, so wear rubber gloves when handling peppers and do not touch your eyes.

1 Heat 1 tablespoon oil in large skillet over medium-high heat. Add bell peppers and onion; cook 5 minutes or until tender and browned in spots, stirring frequently. Transfer to large bowl; stir in 1 tablespoon fajita seasoning mix and 1 tablespoon water.

2 Heat remaining 1 tablespoon oil in same skillet over medium-high heat. Add chicken; cook 7 to 10 minutes or until cooked through, stirring occasionally. Add remaining 1 tablespoon fajita seasoning mix and 1 tablespoon water; cook and stir until chicken is coated.

3 Preheat broiler. Place chips in 11×7-inch baking dish or pan; top with vegetables, chicken, Cheddar and Monterey Jack cheeses and jalapeño pepper.

4 Broil 2 to 4 minutes or until cheeses are melted. Top with lettuce, ½ cup salsa, sour cream and guacamole, if desired. Serve immediately with additional salsa.

PEPPERONI BREAD
MAKES ABOUT 6 SERVINGS

1 package (about 14 ounces) refrigerated pizza dough

8 slices provolone cheese

20 to 30 slices pepperoni (about half of 6-ounce package)

½ teaspoon Italian seasoning

¾ cup (3 ounces) shredded mozzarella cheese

½ cup grated Parmesan cheese

1 egg, beaten

Marinara sauce, heated

1 Preheat oven to 400°F. Unroll pizza dough on sheet of parchment paper with long side in front of you. Cut off corners of dough to create oval shape.

2 Arrange half of provolone slices over bottom half of oval, cutting to fit as necessary. Top with pepperoni; sprinkle with ¼ teaspoon Italian seasoning. Top with mozzarella, Parmesan and remaining provolone slices; sprinkle with remaining ¼ teaspoon Italian seasoning.

3 Fold top half of dough over filling to create half moon (calzone) shape; press edges with fork or pinch edges to seal. Transfer calzone with parchment paper to large baking sheet; curve slightly into crescent shape. Brush with beaten egg.

4 Bake about 16 minutes or until crust is golden brown. Remove to wire rack to cool slightly. Cut crosswise into slices; serve warm with marinara sauce.

PEPPERONI STUFFED MUSHROOMS

MAKES 4 TO 6 SERVINGS

16 medium mushrooms

1 tablespoon olive oil

½ cup finely chopped onion

2 ounces pepperoni, finely chopped (about ½ cup)

¼ cup finely chopped green bell pepper

½ teaspoon seasoned salt

¼ teaspoon dried oregano

⅛ teaspoon black pepper

½ cup crushed buttery crackers (about 12)

¼ cup grated Parmesan cheese

1 tablespoon chopped fresh parsley, plus additional for garnish

1. Preheat oven to 350°F. Line baking sheet with foil; spray foil with nonstick cooking spray.

2. Clean mushrooms; remove stems and set aside caps. Finely chop stems.

3. Heat oil in large skillet over medium-high heat. Add onion; cook and stir 2 to 3 minutes or until softened. Add mushroom stems, pepperoni, bell pepper, seasoned salt, oregano and black pepper; cook and stir about 5 minutes or until vegetables are tender but not browned.

4. Remove from heat; stir in crushed crackers, cheese and 1 tablespoon parsley until blended. Spoon mixture into mushroom caps, mounding slightly in centers. Place filled caps on prepared baking sheet.

5. Bake about 20 minutes or until heated through. Garnish with additional parsley.

PEPPERONI PIZZA ROLLS
MAKES 12 ROLLS

1 loaf (16 ounces) frozen pizza dough or white bread dough, thawed according to package directions

½ cup pizza sauce, plus additional sauce for serving

⅓ cup chopped pepperoni or mini pepperoni slices (half of 2½-ounce package)

9 to 10 slices fontina, provolone or provolone-mozzarella blend cheese*

For best results, use thinner cheese slices which are less than 1 ounce each.

1 Spray 12 standard (2½-inch) muffin pan cups with nonstick cooking spray.

2 Roll out dough on lightly floured surface into 12×10-inch rectangle. Spread ½ cup pizza sauce over dough, leaving ½-inch border on one long side. Sprinkle with pepperoni; top with cheese, cutting slices to fit as necessary. Starting with long side opposite ½-inch border, roll up dough jelly-roll style; pinch seam to seal.

3 Cut crosswise into 1-inch slices; place slices cut sides up in prepared muffin cups. Cover with plastic wrap; let rise in warm place 30 to 40 minutes or until nearly doubled in size. Preheat oven to 350°F.

4 Bake about 25 minutes or until golden brown. Loosen bottom and sides with small spatula or knife; remove to wire rack. Serve warm with additional sauce for dipping, if desired.

SWEET HOT CHICKEN WINGS

MAKES ABOUT 36 APPETIZERS

- 3 **pounds chicken wings**
- ¾ **cup salsa, plus additional for serving**
- ⅔ **cup honey**
- ⅓ **cup soy sauce**
- ¼ **cup Dijon mustard**
- 2 **tablespoons vegetable oil**
- 1 **tablespoon grated fresh ginger**
- ½ **teaspoon grated orange peel**
- ½ **teaspoon grated lemon peel**

1 Cut off and discard wing tips from chicken. Cut each wing in half at joint. Place wings in 13×9-inch baking dish.

2 Combine ¾ cup salsa, honey, soy sauce, mustard, oil, ginger, orange peel and lemon peel in small bowl; mix well. Pour over wings. Marinate, covered, in refrigerator at least 6 hours or overnight.

3 Preheat oven to 400°F. Place wings in single layer on foil-lined, 15×10-inch jelly-roll pan. Pour marinade evenly over wings. Bake 40 to 45 minutes until brown. Serve warm with additional salsa and garnish, if desired.

WARM CRAB AND BEER DIP

MAKES 8 SERVINGS

12 ounces cream cheese, softened

½ cup finely chopped red bell pepper

½ cup mayonnaise

½ cup beer

¼ cup finely chopped onion

¼ cup chopped fresh parsley

1 egg

1 teaspoon hot pepper sauce

¼ teaspoon salt

12 ounces crabmeat*

Pita chips

Pick out and discard any shell or cartilage from crabmeat.

1 Preheat oven to 375°F. Spray 1-quart baking dish with nonstick cooking spray.

2 Combine cream cheese, bell pepper, mayonnaise, beer, onion, parsley, egg, hot pepper sauce and salt in medium bowl; mix well. Fold in crabmeat. Spoon into prepared baking dish.

3 Bake 35 minutes or until bubbly and browned on top. Let stand 10 minutes. Serve with pita chips.

BAD ASS BREAKFASTS

CHOCOLATE-CRANBERRY PUMPKIN PANCAKES

MAKES 16 TO 18 (4-INCH) PANCAKES

- 2 cups all-purpose flour
- ⅓ cup packed brown sugar
- 2 teaspoons baking powder
- ½ teaspoon salt
- ½ teaspoon ground cinnamon
- ¼ teaspoon baking soda
- ¼ teaspoon ground ginger
- ¼ teaspoon ground nutmeg
- 1½ cups milk
- 2 eggs
- ½ cup solid-pack pumpkin
- ¼ cup vegetable oil
- ½ cup mini semisweet chocolate chips
- ½ cup dried cranberries
- ⅓ cup cinnamon chips
- 1 to 2 teaspoons butter, plus additional for serving
  Maple syrup

1 Combine flour, brown sugar, baking powder, salt, cinnamon, baking soda, ginger and nutmeg in large bowl; mix well. Beat milk, eggs, pumpkin and oil in medium bowl until well blended. Add to flour mixture with chocolate chips, cranberries and cinnamon chips; stir just until dry ingredients are moistened.

2 Heat 1 teaspoon butter on griddle over medium heat. Pour batter by ¼ cupfuls onto griddle. Cook until bubbles form and bottom of pancakes are lightly browned; turn and cook 2 minutes or until browned and cooked through. Repeat with remaining batter, adding additional butter to griddle if necessary. Serve with maple syrup and additional butter, if desired.

CHOCOLATE DOUGHNUTS

MAKES 14 TO 16 DOUGHNUTS

2¼ cups all-purpose flour

½ cup unsweetened cocoa powder

¼ cup cornstarch

1 teaspoon salt

1 teaspoon baking powder

½ teaspoon baking soda

½ teaspoon ground cinnamon

½ teaspoon ground nutmeg

1 cup granulated sugar

2 eggs

¼ cup (½ stick) butter, melted

¼ cup applesauce

1 teaspoon vanilla

½ cup buttermilk

Vegetable oil for frying

GLAZE

½ cup milk

1 cup semisweet or dark chocolate chips

½ teaspoon vanilla

1½ to 2 cups powdered sugar, sifted

Multicolored sprinkles

1 Whisk flour, cocoa, cornstarch, salt, baking powder, baking soda, cinnamon and nutmeg in large bowl.

2 Beat 1 cup granulated sugar and eggs in large bowl with electric mixer on high speed 3 minutes or until pale and thick. Stir in butter, applesauce and vanilla. Add flour mixture alternately with buttermilk, mixing on low speed after each addition. Press plastic wrap directly onto surface of dough; refrigerate at least 1 hour.

3 Pour about 2 inches of oil into Dutch oven or large heavy saucepan; clip deep-fry or candy thermometer to side of pot. Heat over medium-high heat to 360°F to 370°F.

4 Meanwhile, generously flour work surface. Turn out dough onto work surface and dust top with flour. Roll dough to about ¼-inch thickness; cut out doughnuts with floured doughnut cutter. Gather and reroll scraps. Line large wire rack with paper towels.

5 Working in batches, add doughnuts to hot oil. Cook 1 minute per side or until golden brown. Do not crowd the pan and adjust heat to maintain temperature during frying. Cool on wire racks.

6 For glaze, heat milk in small saucepan until bubbles form around edge of pan. Remove from heat. Add chocolate chips; let stand 1 minute to soften. Add vanilla; whisk until smooth. Whisk in enough powdered sugar to form stiff glaze. Dip tops of doughnuts in glaze; top with sprinkles. Let stand until glaze is set.

MAPLE PECAN GRANOLA
MAKES ABOUT 6 CUPS

- ¼ cup maple syrup
- ¼ cup packed dark brown sugar
- 1½ teaspoons vanilla
- ½ teaspoon ground cinnamon
- ½ teaspoon coarse salt
- 6 tablespoons vegetable oil
- 3 cups old-fashioned rolled oats
- 1½ cups pecans, coarsely chopped
- ¾ cup shredded coconut
- ¼ cup ground flax seeds
- ¼ cup water
- Plain yogurt or milk (optional)

1 Preheat oven to 350°F. Line large rimmed baking sheet with parchment paper.

2 Whisk maple syrup, brown sugar, vanilla, cinnamon, salt and oil in large bowl until blended. Add oats, pecans, coconut and flax seeds; stir until evenly coated. Stir in water. Spread mixture on prepared baking sheet, pressing into even layer.

3 Bake 30 minutes or until granola is golden brown and fragrant. Cool completely on baking sheet. Serve with yogurt or milk, if desired. Store leftovers in an airtight container at room temperature 1 month.

NOTE

For chunky granola, do not stir during baking. For loose granola, stir every 10 minutes during baking.

RICH AND GOOEY CINNAMON BUNS

MAKES 12 BUNS

DOUGH

- 1 package (¼ ounce) active dry yeast
- 1 cup warm milk (110°F)
- 2 eggs, beaten
- ½ cup granulated sugar
- ¼ cup (½ stick) butter, softened
- 1 teaspoon salt
- 4 to 4¼ cups all-purpose flour

FILLING

- 1 cup packed brown sugar
- 3 tablespoons ground cinnamon
  Pinch of salt
- 6 tablespoons (¾ stick) butter, softened

ICING

- 1½ cups powdered sugar
- 3 ounces cream cheese, softened
- ¼ cup (½ stick) butter, softened
- ½ teaspoon vanilla
- ⅛ teaspoon salt

1 Dissolve yeast in warm milk in large bowl of electric mixer. Add eggs, granulated sugar, ¼ cup butter and 1 teaspoon salt; beat at medium speed until well blended. Add 4 cups flour; beat at low speed until dough begins to come together. Knead dough with dough hook at low speed about 5 minutes or until smooth, elastic and slightly sticky. Add additional flour, 1 tablespoon at a time, if necessary to prevent sticking.

2 Shape dough into a ball. Place in large greased bowl; turn to grease top. Cover and let rise in warm place about 1 hour or until doubled in size. Meanwhile, for filling, combine brown sugar, cinnamon and pinch of salt in small bowl; mix well.

3 Spray 13×9-inch baking pan with nonstick cooking spray. Roll out dough into 18×14-inch rectangle on floured surface. Spread 6 tablespoons butter evenly over dough; top with cinnamon-sugar mixture. Beginning with long side, roll up dough tightly jelly-roll style; pinch seam to seal. Cut log crosswise into 12 slices; place slices cut sides up in prepared pan. Cover and let rise in warm place about 30 minutes or until almost doubled in size. Preheat oven to 350°F.

4 Bake 20 to 25 minutes or until golden brown. Meanwhile, for icing, combine powdered sugar, cream cheese, ¼ cup butter, vanilla and ⅛ teaspoon salt in medium bowl; beat with electric mixer at medium speed 2 minutes or until smooth and creamy. Spread icing generously over warm cinnamon buns.

SPICY SAUSAGE POPOVER PIZZA

MAKES 8 SERVINGS

½ pound turkey breakfast sausage patties, crumbled

½ pound ground turkey

⅓ cup chopped onion

1 clove garlic, minced

¾ cup chopped red bell pepper

1½ cups all-purpose flour

¼ teaspoon salt

¼ teaspoon red pepper flakes

1 cup milk

3 eggs

1 cup (4 ounces) shredded Cheddar cheese

½ cup (2 ounces) shredded mozzarella cheese

½ cup pizza sauce

1 Preheat oven to 425°F. Generously spray 13×9-inch baking dish with nonstick cooking spray.

2 Combine sausage, ground turkey, onion and garlic in large skillet; cook and stir over medium heat until turkey is browned. Drain fat. Stir in bell pepper.

3 Combine flour, salt and red pepper flakes in medium bowl. Combine milk and eggs in another medium bowl; whisk into flour mixture until smooth. Pour into prepared baking dish. Sprinkle sausage mixture over top. Sprinkle with cheeses.

4 Bake 21 to 23 minutes or until puffed and golden brown. Cut into 8 rectangles.

5 Meanwhile, microwave pizza sauce on HIGH 1 minute. Top pizza with pizza sauce.

COCONUT BUTTERSCOTCH DOUGHNUTS

MAKES 12 DOUGHNUTS

- 1 cup all-purpose flour
- ½ cup sugar
- 2 tablespoons cornstarch
- 1½ teaspoons baking powder
- ½ teaspoon baking soda
- ½ teaspoon salt
- ¼ cup butterscotch chips
- ¼ cup flaked coconut
- ½ cup buttermilk
- ¼ cup (½ stick) butter, melted
- 1 egg
- ½ teaspoon vanilla

TOPPING

- ¼ cup whipping cream
- ½ cup butterscotch chips
- ½ cup flaked coconut,* toasted
- ¼ cup bittersweet chocolate chips, melted

To toast coconut, spread evenly on ungreased baking sheet. Toast in preheated 350°F oven 5 to 7 minutes, stirring occasionally, until light golden brown.

1 Preheat oven to 425°F. Spray 12 cavities of doughnut pan with nonstick cooking spray.

2 Combine flour, sugar, cornstarch, baking powder, baking soda and salt in medium bowl; mix well. Add ¼ cup butterscotch chips and ¼ cup coconut; toss to coat. Whisk buttermilk, butter, egg and vanilla in medium bowl until well blended. Stir into flour mixture just until blended.

3 Spoon batter into medium resealable food storage bag. Cut ½-inch corner from bag. Pipe mixture evenly into prepared cups, filling half full.

4 Bake about 7 minutes or until doughnuts are puffed and golden. Cool in pan on wire rack 3 to 5 minutes. Remove to wire rack; cool completely.

5 For glaze, heat cream in small saucepan over medium-low heat until bubbles form around edge of pan. Add ½ cup butterscotch chips; whisk until melted and smooth. Let cool slightly. Dip tops of doughnuts in glaze; place on wire rack. Dip tops again; immediately sprinkle with toasted coconut. Drizzle with melted chocolate.

BACON & POTATO FRITTATA

MAKES 4 TO 6 SERVINGS

5 eggs

½ cup bacon, crisp-cooked and crumbled

¼ cup half-and-half or milk

⅛ teaspoon salt

⅛ teaspoon black pepper

3 tablespoons butter

2 cups frozen O'Brien hash brown potatoes with onions and peppers

1 Preheat broiler. Beat eggs in medium bowl. Add bacon, half-and-half, salt and pepper; beat until well blended.

2 Melt butter in large ovenproof skillet over medium-high heat. Add potatoes; cook and stir 4 minutes. Pour egg mixture into skillet. Reduce heat to medium; cover and cook 6 minutes or until eggs are set at edges (top will still be wet).

3 Transfer skillet to broiler. Broil 4 inches from heat source 1 to 2 minutes or until top is golden brown and center is set.

SERVING SUGGESTION

Top frittata with red bell pepper strips, chopped fresh chives and salsa.

CHOW DOWN BOWLS

DUBLIN CODDLE
MAKES 6 SERVINGS

8 ounces Irish bacon*

8 pork sausages, preferably Irish bangers

3 onions, sliced

Black pepper

2 pounds potatoes, peeled and thickly sliced

2 carrots, peeled and cut into 1½-inch pieces

¼ cup chopped fresh parsley, plus additional for garnish

2 sprigs fresh thyme

3 cups chicken broth or water

Or substitute Canadian bacon or pancetta.

1 Cook bacon in Dutch oven over medium heat until crisp. Remove to paper towel-lined plate; cut into 1-inch pieces. Drain all but 1 tablespoon drippings.

2 Add sausages to Dutch oven; cook about 10 minutes or until browned on all sides. Remove to paper towel-lined plate; cut into 1-inch pieces.

3 Add onions to Dutch oven; cook and stir about 8 minutes or until translucent. Return bacon and sausages to Dutch oven; sprinkle with pepper. Add potatoes, carrots, ¼ cup parsley and thyme; sprinkle generously with pepper. Pour broth over vegetables; bring to a boil.

4 Reduce heat to low; partially cover and simmer about 1 hour 20 minutes or until vegetables are tender. Sprinkle with additional parsley, if desired.

OXTAIL SOUP WITH BEER

MAKES 4 SERVINGS

- 2½ pounds oxtails (beef or veal)
- 1 large onion, sliced
- 4 carrots, cut into 1-inch pieces, divided
- 3 stalks celery, cut into 1-inch pieces, divided
- 2 sprigs fresh parsley
- 5 whole black peppercorns
- 1 bay leaf
- 4 cups beef broth
- 1 cup dark beer or stout
- 2 large diced baking potatoes
- 1 teaspoon salt
- 2 tablespoons chopped fresh parsley (optional)

1 Combine oxtails, onion, half of carrots, one third of celery, parsley sprigs, peppercorns and bay leaf in large saucepan. Add broth and beer; bring to a boil over high heat. Reduce heat to low; cover and simmer 3 hours or until meat is falling off bones.

2 Remove oxtails to plate; set aside. Strain broth and return to saucepan; skim fat. Add remaining carrots, celery and potatoes; bring to a simmer. Cook 10 to 15 minutes or until vegetables are tender.

3 Remove meat from oxtails; discard bones. Stir meat and salt into soup; cook until heated through. Sprinkle with chopped parsley, if desired.

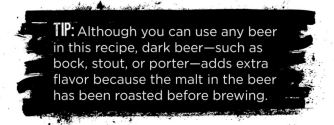

TIP: Although you can use any beer in this recipe, dark beer—such as bock, stout, or porter—adds extra flavor because the malt in the beer has been roasted before brewing.

RICH AND HEARTY DRUMSTICK SOUP

MAKES 8 SERVINGS

- 2 turkey drumsticks (about 1¾ pounds)
- 3 carrots, sliced
- 3 stalks celery, thinly sliced
- 1 onion, chopped
- 2 cloves garlic, minced
- 1 teaspoon poultry seasoning
- 4 cups reduced-sodium chicken broth
- 3 cups water
- 8 ounces uncooked egg noodles
- ⅓ cup chopped fresh Italian parsley
- Salt and black pepper

SLOW COOKER DIRECTIONS

1 Combine drumsticks, carrots, celery, onion, garlic and poultry seasoning in slow cooker. Pour broth and water over top. Cover; cook on HIGH 5 hours or until meat is falling off the bones.

2 Remove turkey; set aside. Add noodles to slow cooker. Cover; cook 30 minutes or until tender. Meanwhile, remove and discard skin and bones from turkey; shred meat.

3 Return turkey to slow cooker. Cover; cook until heated through. Stir in parsley. Season with salt and pepper.

GRILLED STEAK CHILI
MAKES 10 TO 12 SERVINGS

¼ cup minced garlic

¼ cup corn oil

3 cups chopped onion

3 cans (about 14 ounces each) Mexican-style diced tomatoes with chiles

2 cans (about 14 ounces each) crushed tomatoes

2 cups beef broth

¼ cup plus 2 tablespoons chili powder

2 teaspoons ground cumin

2 teaspoons dried oregano

1 teaspoon ground black pepper

4 pounds beef steak (preferably rib-eye)

¼ cup masa harina (corn flour) or yellow cornmeal (optional)

Minced fresh cilantro, sliced green onions and sliced black olives (optional)

1 Combine garlic and oil in Dutch oven over low heat; cook 1 minute. Add onion; cook and stir over medium heat 5 minutes. Stir in tomatoes, broth, chili powder, cumin, oregano and pepper; bring to a boil, stirring occasionally. Reduce heat; cover and simmer 1 to 2 hours or until thick.

2 Preheat grill or broiler. Grill steak about 8 minutes or until just browned on both sides. Let stand 15 minutes. Cut steak into 2×½-inch strips on rimmed cutting board. Stir steak and accumulated juices into chili. Cook 5 to 10 minutes. For thicker chili, slowly add masa harina; cook and stir 12 to 15 minutes or until thickened. Garnish with cilantro, green onions and olives.

CHEESY POTATO CHOWDER

MAKES 6 SERVINGS

1½ cups water

3 unpeeled medium red potatoes, cubed

1 stalk celery, sliced

1 medium carrot, chopped

¼ cup (½ stick) butter or margarine

3 green onions, sliced

¼ cup all-purpose flour

1 teaspoon salt

⅛ teaspoon black pepper

4 cups milk

2 cups (8 ounces) shredded American cheese

1 cup (4 ounces) shredded Swiss cheese

½ teaspoon caraway seeds

   Oyster crackers (optional)

1 Combine water, potatoes, celery and carrot in medium saucepan. Bring to a boil over high heat. Reduce heat to low; simmer 10 minutes or until vegetables are tender.

2 Meanwhile, melt butter in large saucepan over medium heat. Add green onions; cook and stir 2 minutes or until tender. Add flour, salt and pepper; cook and stir 1 minute.

3 Stir milk and potato mixture into flour mixture; cook and stir over medium heat until bubbly. Reduce heat to low; stir in cheeses and caraway seeds. Simmer just until heated through and cheeses are melted, stirring constantly. Serve with oyster crackers, if desired.

SPICY SHRIMP GUMBO
MAKES 8 SERVINGS

½ cup vegetable oil

½ cup all-purpose flour

1 large onion, chopped

½ cup chopped fresh parsley

½ cup chopped celery

½ cup sliced green onions

6 cloves garlic, minced

4 cups chicken broth or water*

1 package (10 ounces) frozen sliced okra, thawed (optional)

1 teaspoon salt

½ teaspoon ground red pepper

2 pounds raw medium shrimp, peeled and deveined

3 cups hot cooked rice

Sprigs fresh parsley (optional)

Traditional gumbo is thick is like stew. For thinner gumbo, add 1 to 2 cups additional broth.

1 For roux, blend oil and flour in large heavy stockpot. Cook over medium heat 10 to 15 minutes or until roux is dark brown but not burned, stirring often.

2 Add chopped onion, chopped parsley, celery, green onions and garlic to roux. Cook over medium heat 5 to 10 minutes or until vegetables are tender. Add broth, okra, salt and red pepper. Cover; simmer 15 minutes.

3 Add shrimp; simmer 3 to 5 minutes or until shrimp turn pink and opaque.

4 Place about ⅓ cup rice into 8 wide-rimmed soup bowls; top with gumbo. Garnish with parsley sprigs, if desired.

CLASSIC FRENCH ONION SOUP

MAKES 4 SERVINGS

- 4 tablespoons (½ stick) butter
- 3 large yellow onions, sliced
- 1 cup dry white wine
- 3 cans (about 14 ounces each) beef or chicken broth
- 1 teaspoon Worcestershire sauce
- ½ teaspoon salt
- ½ teaspoon dried thyme
- 4 slices French bread, toasted
- 1 cup (4 ounces) shredded Swiss cheese

  Fresh thyme (optional)

SLOW COOKER DIRECTIONS

1 Melt butter in large skillet over medium heat. Add onions, cook and stir 15 minutes or until onions are soft and lightly browned. Stir in wine.

2 Combine onion mixture, broth, Worcestershire sauce, salt and dried thyme in slow cooker. Cover; cook on LOW 4 to 4½ hours.

3 Ladle soup into 4 heatproof bowls; top with bread slice and cheese. Broil 4 inches from heat 2 to 3 minutes or until cheese is bubbly and browned. Garnish with fresh thyme.

CLASSIC CHILI

MAKES 6 SERVINGS

1½ pounds ground beef

1½ cups chopped onion

1 cup chopped green bell pepper

2 cloves garlic, minced

3 cans (about 15 ounces each) dark red kidney beans, rinsed and drained

2 cans (about 15 ounces each) tomato sauce

1 can (about 14 ounces) diced tomatoes

2 to 3 teaspoons chili powder

1 to 2 teaspoons dry hot mustard

¾ teaspoon dried basil

½ teaspoon black pepper

1 to 2 dried hot chile peppers (optional)

Shredded Cheddar cheese (optional)

Fresh cilantro leaves (optional)

SLOW COOKER DIRECTIONS

1 Cook and stir beef, onion, bell pepper and garlic in large skillet over medium-high heat 6 to 8 minutes or until beef is browned and onion is tender. Drain fat. Transfer to slow cooker.

2 Add beans, tomato sauce, diced tomatoes, chili powder, dry mustard, basil, black pepper and chile peppers, if desired, to slow cooker; mix well. Cover; cook on LOW 8 to 10 hours or on HIGH 4 to 5 hours. Remove and discard chiles before serving. Top with cheese, if desired. Garnish with cilantro.

STOIC SANDWICHES

PULLED PORK SANDWICHES

MAKES 6 TO 8 SERVINGS

- 2 tablespoons kosher salt
- 2 tablespoons packed light brown sugar
- 2 tablespoons paprika
- 1 teaspoon dry mustard
- 1 teaspoon black pepper
- 1 boneless pork shoulder roast (about 3 pounds)
- 1½ cups stout
- ½ cup cider vinegar
- 6 to 8 large hamburger buns, split
- ¾ cup barbecue sauce

1 Preheat oven to 325°F. Combine salt, brown sugar, paprika, dry mustard and pepper in small bowl; mix well. Rub into pork.

2 Place pork in 4-quart Dutch oven. Add stout and vinegar. Cover; bake 3 hours or until meat is fork-tender. Remove to large cutting board. Cool 15 to 30 minutes or until cool enough to handle.

3 Shred pork into pieces with 2 forks. Divide onto buns; serve warm with barbecue sauce.

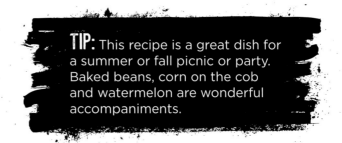

TIP: This recipe is a great dish for a summer or fall picnic or party. Baked beans, corn on the cob and watermelon are wonderful accompaniments.

ITALIAN MEATBALL SUBS

MAKES 4 SERVINGS

½ cup chopped onion

3 teaspoons finely chopped garlic, divided

1 can (about 14 ounces) Italian-style crushed tomatoes, undrained

2 bay leaves

2½ teaspoons dried basil, divided

2 teaspoons dried oregano, divided

¾ teaspoon black pepper, divided

¼ teaspoon red pepper flakes

½ pound 95% lean ground beef

⅓ cup chopped green onions

⅓ cup plain dry bread crumbs

¼ cup chopped fresh parsley

1 egg white

2 tablespoons water

½ teaspoon dried marjoram

½ teaspoon dry mustard

4 French bread rolls, warmed and cut in half lengthwise

1 Spray large saucepan with nonstick cooking spray; heat over medium heat. Add onion and 2 teaspoons garlic; cook and stir 5 minutes or until onion is tender. Add tomatoes, bay leaves, 2 teaspoons basil, 1 teaspoon oregano, ½ teaspoon black pepper and red pepper flakes; cover and simmer 30 minutes, stirring occasionally.

2 Combine beef, green onions, bread crumbs, parsley, egg white, water, remaining 1 teaspoon garlic, ½ teaspoon basil, 1 teaspoon oregano, ¼ teaspoon black pepper, marjoram and dry mustard in medium bowl; mix well. Shape into 16 meatballs.

3 Spray large nonstick skillet with cooking spray; heat over medium heat. Add meatballs; cook 5 minutes or until meatballs are cooked through (160°F), turning occasionally.

4 Remove and discard bay leaves from tomato sauce. Add meatballs; cook 5 minutes, stirring occasionally.

5 Place 4 meatballs in each roll. Spoon additional sauce over meatballs. Serve immediately.

SPICY ONION STEAK SANDWICHES

MAKES 4 SERVINGS

1 cup barbecue sauce

3 tablespoons chipotle salsa*

1 tablespoon vegetable oil

1 large onion, sliced

1 pound sandwich steaks,** cut into wide strips

4 sub rolls, split

8 slices sharp white Cheddar or Monterey Jack cheese

Chipotle salsa is a canned mixture of finely chopped chipotle peppers in adobo sauce. Look for it in the Latin foods section of the supermarket.

**You may substitute 1 pound thick-sliced deli roast beef for the sandwich steaks. Omit step 3.*

1 Combine barbecue sauce and chipotle salsa in small bowl. Reserve ½ cup mixture.

2 Heat oil in large nonstick skillet over medium heat. Add onion; cook and stir 10 minutes or until lightly browned. Add barbecue sauce mixture; toss to combine. Remove from heat.

3 Heat nonstick grill pan over high heat. Cook steak strips 2 minutes on each side.

4 Brush reserved sauce evenly onto rolls. Divide onion, steak and cheese slices evenly among rolls.

GRILLED REUBENS WITH COLESLAW

MAKES 4 SERVINGS

2 cups sauerkraut

¼ cup (½ stick) butter, softened

8 slices marble rye or rye bread

12 ounces thinly sliced deli corned beef or pastrami

¼ to ½ cup Thousand Island dressing

4 slices Swiss cheese

2 cups deli coleslaw

4 kosher garlic pickle spears

1 Preheat indoor grill or large grill pan. Drain sauerkraut well on paper towels.

2 Spread butter evenly over one side of each slice of bread. Turn 4 bread slices over; top evenly with corned beef, 1 to 2 tablespoons dressing, sauerkraut and cheese. Top with remaining 4 bread slices, butter side up.

3 Grill 4 minutes or just until cheese begins to melt. Serve with coleslaw and pickles.

NOTE

'Stack sandwich ingredients in the order given to prevent sogginess.

CHICKEN BURGERS WITH WHITE CHEDDAR

MAKES 4 SERVINGS

1¼ pounds ground chicken

1 cup plain dry bread crumbs

½ cup diced red bell pepper

½ cup ground walnuts

¼ cup sliced green onions

¼ cup light beer

2 tablespoons chopped fresh parsley

2 tablespoons lemon juice

2 cloves garlic, minced

¾ teaspoon salt

⅛ teaspoon black pepper

4 slices white Cheddar cheese

4 whole wheat buns

Dijon mustard and lettuce leaves

1 Combine chicken, bread crumbs, bell pepper, walnuts, green onions, beer, parsley, lemon juice, garlic, salt and black pepper in large bowl; mix lightly. Shape into 4 patties.

2 Spray large skillet with nonstick cooking spray; heat over medium-high heat. Cook patties 6 to 7 minutes on each side or until cooked through (165°F). Place cheese on patties; cover skillet just until cheese melts.

3 Serve burgers on buns with mustard and lettuce.

SPICY PORK PO' BOYS

MAKES 4 SERVINGS

- 2 tablespoons chili powder
- 1 tablespoon salt
- 1 tablespoon onion powder
- 1 tablespoon garlic powder
- 1 tablespoon paprika
- 1 tablespoon black pepper
- 1 teaspoon ground red pepper
- 1 pound boneless pork ribs
- ½ cup cola beverage
- 1 tablespoon hot pepper sauce
- Dash Worcestershire sauce
- ½ cup ketchup
- 4 French rolls, toasted
- ½ cup prepared coleslaw

1 Combine chili powder, salt, onion powder, garlic powder, paprika, black pepper and red pepper in small bowl. Rub mixture over pork, coating all sides. Cover and refrigerate at least 3 hours or overnight.

2 Preheat oven to 250°F. Place pork in Dutch oven. Combine cola, hot pepper sauce and Worcestershire sauce in small bowl; drizzle evenly over pork.

3 Cover and bake about 4 hours or until pork is fork-tender. Remove to large bowl. Stir ketchup into Dutch oven; cook 4 to 6 minutes or until sauce has thickened, stirring frequently. Pour sauce over pork, pulling meat apart with 2 forks and coating with sauce. Serve on rolls with coleslaw.

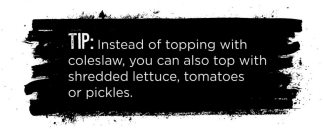

TIP: Instead of topping with coleslaw, you can also top with shredded lettuce, tomatoes or pickles.

HONEY-MUSTARD AND BEER PULLED PORK SANDWICHES

MAKES 8 SERVINGS

- 1 tablespoon chili powder
- 2 teaspoons ground cumin
- ½ teaspoon salt
- 2 tablespoons yellow mustard
- 2 pounds bone-in pork shoulder roast
- 2 bottles (12 ounces each) beer, divided
- ¾ cup ketchup
- 3 tablespoons honey
- 2 tablespoons cider vinegar
- 8 soft sandwich rolls
- 24 bread and butter pickle chips

1 Prepare grill for indirect cooking over medium-low heat.

2 Combine chili powder, cumin and salt in small bowl. Spread mustard on all sides of pork, then cover evenly with cumin mixture. Transfer pork to rack in disposable foil pan. Reserve ¾ cup beer. Pour enough remaining beer into foil pan to just cover rack beneath pork. Place tray on grid opposite heat source. Grill, covered, 4 to 6 hours or until internal temperature reaches 160°F. Remove to cutting board, tent with foil and let stand 15 minutes.

3 Combine reserved ¾ cup beer, ketchup, honey and vinegar in small saucepan. Bring to a boil over medium-high heat. Reduce heat to medium; cook and stir until thickened.

4 Shred pork with 2 forks, discarding any bone, fat or connective tissue. Combine pork and sauce in medium bowl; toss gently to combine. Serve on rolls with pickles.

PASTRAMI REUBEN SANDWICHES WITH BEER KRAUT

MAKES 4 SERVINGS

- 1 tablespoon canola oil
- ½ cup thinly sliced Vidalia or other sweet onion
- 1 cup well-drained sauerkraut
- 1 teaspoon sugar
- ½ cup beer
  Unsalted butter, softened
- 8 slices rye bread
- ½ cup Russian dressing
- 4 slices Swiss cheese
- 1 pound thinly sliced pastrami

1 Heat oil in medium skillet over medium-high heat. Add onion; cook and stir 2 minutes or until slightly softened. Add sauerkraut and sugar; cook 3 minutes. Pour in beer; cook 3 minutes or until evaporated, stirring occasionally. Remove from heat.

2 Butter one side of bread slices. Place 4 slices bread, butter side down, on work surface. Spread with 1 tablespoon Russian dressing. Top with one fourth of sauerkraut mixture, 1 slice Swiss cheese and one fourth of pastrami. Spread unbuttered sides of remaining 4 slices bread with remaining Russian dressing; place butter side up on pastrami.

3 Heat large nonstick skillet over medium heat. Place 2 sandwiches in skillet; press firmly with spatula. Cook 3 minutes or until bread is golden. Turn; place second large skillet on top of sandwiches and press firmly. Cook 4 minutes or until golden. Repeat with remaining 2 sandwiches.

SPICY ITALIAN BEEF
MAKES 8 TO 10 SERVINGS

- 1 boneless beef chuck roast (3 to 4 pounds)
- 1 jar (12 ounces) peperoncini
- 1 can (about 14 ounces) beef broth
- 1 bottle (12 ounces) beer
- 1 onion, minced
- 2 tablespoons Italian seasoning
- 1 loaf French bread, cut into thick slices
- 10 slices provolone cheese (optional)

SLOW COOKER DIRECTIONS

1 Trim fat from roast. Cut roast, if necessary, to fit into slow cooker.

2 Drain peperoncini. Pull off stem ends and discard. Add peperoncini, broth, beer, onion and Italian seasoning to slow cooker; *do not stir.* Cover; cook on LOW 8 to 10 hours.

3 Remove meat from slow cooker to large cutting board; shred with 2 forks. Return shredded meat to slow cooker; mix well. Serve meat mixture on French bread; top with cheese, if desired. Serve with sauce and peperoncini, if desired.

TIP: Peperoncini are thin, 2- to 3-inch-long, pickled mild peppers. Look for them in the Italian foods or pickled foods section of the grocery store.

SPICY MEATBALL SANDWICHES

MAKES 6 SANDWICHES

1 large (17×15-inch) foil cooking bag

1 jar (26 ounces) marinara sauce

1 pound frozen precooked Italian-style meatballs

½ cup chopped green bell pepper

⅓ cup sliced black olives

2 teaspoons Italian seasoning

¼ teaspoon ground red pepper

6 slices mozzarella cheese, halved lengthwise

6 hoagie buns

3 tablespoons finely shredded Parmesan cheese

1 Prepare grill for direct cooking.

2 Place foil bag on baking sheet. Combine marinara sauce, meatballs, bell pepper, olives, Italian seasoning and red pepper in large bowl. Pour into bag. Double fold open side of bag, leaving head space for heat circulation.

3 Slide bag off baking sheet onto grill grid. Grill, covered, over medium-high coals 11 to 13 minutes or until meatballs are hot. Carefully open bag to allow steam to escape.

4 Meanwhile, place 2 pieces mozzarella cheese on bottom of each bun. Spoon meatball mixture onto buns. Sprinkle with Parmesan cheese.

BBQ ROAST BEEF ➲
MAKES 10 TO 12 SANDWICHES

2 pounds boneless cooked roast beef

1 bottle (12 ounces) barbecue sauce

1½ cups water

10 to 12 sandwich rolls, split

SLOW COOKER DIRECTIONS

1 Combine beef, barbecue sauce and water in slow cooker. Cover; cook on LOW 2 hours. Remove to large cutting board.

2 To serve, shred with 2 forks and place on rolls.

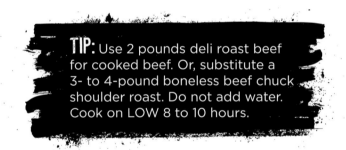

TIP: Use 2 pounds deli roast beef for cooked beef. Or, substitute a 3- to 4-pound boneless beef chuck shoulder roast. Do not add water. Cook on LOW 8 to 10 hours.

OPEN-FACED STEAK AND BLUE CHEESE SANDWICHES
MAKES 4 SERVINGS

4 boneless beef top loin (strip) or tenderloin steaks, cut ¾-inch thick

Black pepper

1 teaspoon olive oil

4 slices ciabatta bread

Salt

8 thin slices blue cheese

1 Season steaks with pepper. Heat oil in large nonstick skillet over medium heat.

2 Add steaks to skillet; do not crowd. Cook 10 to 12 minutes or until medium rare (145°F), turning once. Remove to cutting board. Tent with foil; let stand 5 to 10 minutes.

3 Meanwhile, toast bread. Cut steaks into slices; season with salt. Place 2 slices blue cheese on each toast slice; top with steak slices. Serve immediately.

TAVERN BURGER ➡

MAKES 8 SERVINGS

2 pounds 95% lean
   ground beef
½ cup ketchup
¼ cup packed brown
   sugar
¼ cup yellow mustard
   Hamburger buns

SLOW COOKER DIRECTIONS

1 Brown beef in medium skillet over medium-high heat
  6 to 8 minutes, stirring to break up meat. Drain fat.
  Transfer beef to slow cooker.

2 Add ketchup, brown sugar and mustard to slow
  cooker; mix well. Cover; cook on LOW 4 to 6 hours.
  Serve on buns.

GRILLED VEGETABLE & CHEESE SANDWICHES

MAKES 4 SERVINGS

2 large zucchini, cut
   lengthwise into
   eight ¼-inch slices
4 slices sweet onion
   (such as Vidalia or
   Walla Walla), cut
   ¼ inch thick
1 large yellow bell
   pepper, cut
   lengthwise into
   quarters
6 tablespoons light
   or regular Caesar
   salad dressing,
   divided
8 oval slices
   sourdough bread
6 slices (1 ounce each)
   Muenster cheese

1 Prepare grill for direct cooking. Brush vegetables with
  ¼ cup dressing. Place vegetables on grid over medium
  coals. Grill on covered grill 5 minutes. Turn; grill
  2 minutes.

2 Brush both sides of bread lightly with remaining
  2 tablespoons dressing. Place bread around vegetables;
  grill 2 minutes or until bread is lightly toasted. Turn
  bread; top 4 pieces of bread with 4 slices of cheese.
  Tear remaining 2 cheese slices into small pieces; place
  on bread around cheese. Grill vegetables and bread
  1 to 2 minutes more or until cheese is melted, bread
  is toasted and vegetables are crisp-tender.

3 Arrange vegetables over cheese side of bread; top
  with remaining bread.

SERVING SUGGESTION

Serve with a fresh fruit salad.

HELL OF A MEAL

RESTAURANT-STYLE BABY BACK RIBS

MAKES 4 SERVINGS

- 1¼ cups water
- 1 cup white vinegar
- ⅔ cup packed dark brown sugar
- ½ cup tomato paste
- 1 tablespoon yellow mustard
- 1½ teaspoons salt
- 1 teaspoon liquid smoke
- 1 teaspoon onion powder
- ½ teaspoon garlic powder
- ½ teaspoon paprika
- 2 racks pork baby back ribs (3½ to 4 pounds total)

1 Combine water, vinegar, brown sugar, tomato paste, mustard, salt, liquid smoke, onion powder, garlic powder and paprika in medium saucepan; bring to a boil over medium heat. Reduce heat to medium-low; cook 40 minutes or until sauce thickens, stirring occasionally.

2 Preheat oven to 300°F. Place each rack of ribs on large sheet of heavy-duty foil. Brush some of sauce over ribs, covering completely. Fold down edges of foil tightly to seal and create packet; arrange packets on baking sheet, seam sides up.

3 Bake 2 hours. Prepare grill or preheat broiler. Carefully remove ribs from foil; drain off excess liquid.

4 Brush ribs with sauce; grill or broil about 5 minutes per side or until beginning to char, brushing with sauce again during grilling. Serve with remaining sauce.

SOUTHERN BUTTERMILK FRIED CHICKEN

MAKES 4 SERVINGS

- 2 cups all-purpose flour
- 1½ teaspoons celery salt
- 1 teaspoon dried thyme
- ¾ teaspoon black pepper
- ½ teaspoon dried marjoram
- 1¾ cups buttermilk
- 2 cups vegetable oil
- 3 pounds chicken pieces

1 Combine flour, celery salt, thyme, pepper and marjoram in shallow bowl. Pour buttermilk into medium bowl.

2 Heat oil in heavy deep skillet over medium heat until 350°F on deep-fry thermometer.

3 Dip chicken into buttermilk, 1 piece at a time; shake off excess. Coat with flour mixture; shake off excess. Dip again in buttermilk and coat once more with flour mixture. Fry chicken in batches, skin side down, 10 to 12 minutes or until browned. Turn and fry 12 to 14 minutes or until cooked through (165°F). *Allow temperature of oil to return to 350°F between batches.* Drain chicken on paper towels.

NOTE

Carefully monitor the temperature of the vegetable oil during cooking. It should not drop below 325°F or go higher than 350°F. The chicken can also be cooked in a deep fryer following the manufacturer's directions. Never leave hot oil unattended.

GRILLED STEAK AND BLACK BEAN TACOS
MAKES 4 SERVINGS

1 teaspoon ground cumin

1 teaspoon chili powder

1 teaspoon garlic salt

12 ounces skirt steak, trimmed of fat

4 slices red onion (¼ inch thick)

2 cloves garlic, minced

1 cup canned no-salt-added black beans, rinsed and drained

½ cup salsa

½ cup chopped fresh tomato

8 corn tortillas, warmed

½ cup chopped fresh cilantro

Lime wedges and lime juice (optional)

1 Prepare grill for direct cooking. Combine cumin, chili powder and garlic salt in small bowl; sprinkle evenly over both sides of steak. Coat steak and onion slices lightly with nonstick cooking spray.

2 Grill steak and onions, covered, over medium-high heat 4 to 5 minutes per side or until steak is barely pink in center and onion is tender.

3 Spray large skillet with cooking spray; heat over medium heat. Add garlic; cook and stir 30 seconds. Add beans, salsa and tomato; cook and stir 5 minutes or until heated through.

4 Slice steak crosswise into thin strips; separate onion slices into rings. Serve in warm tortillas with salsa mixture and cilantro. Garnish with lime wedges and lime juice, if desired.

BEER DOUGH PEPPERONI PIZZA
MAKES 2 (10-INCH) PIZZAS

- 1 cup lager or pale ale, at room temperature
- 3 tablespoons olive oil
- 1 package (¼ ounce) instant yeast
- 2¾ cups bread flour, plus additional for rolling dough
- 1 teaspoon salt
- 1 cup prepared pizza sauce
- 6 ounces (about 32 to 36) pepperoni slices
- 2 cups (8 ounces) shredded mozzarella cheese
- ¼ cup freshly grated Parmesan cheese

1 Combine lager, oil and yeast in medium bowl. Stir in 1 cup flour and salt. Gradually stir in enough flour to make thick dough. Turn out onto floured work surface. Knead 8 minutes or until smooth, adding flour as necessary to prevent sticking.

2 Shape dough into a ball. Place in lightly oiled medium bowl, turning to coat. Cover with plastic wrap and let rise in warm place about 1 hour or until doubled in size.

3 Preheat oven to 425°F.

4 Divide dough in half. Shape into 2 balls and place on lightly floured work surface; cover with plastic wrap. Let stand 10 minutes. Roll out each ball into 10-inch round. Transfer to ungreased baking sheet. Spread with ½ cup pizza sauce, leaving ½-inch border around edges. Top with half of pepperoni, 1 cup mozzarella and 2 tablespoons Parmesan cheese. Repeat with remaining ingredients.

5 Bake 15 minutes or until crust is golden brown and cheese is bubbly. Let stand 3 minutes before serving.

HEAVY-DUTY MIXER

To make dough in a heavy-duty mixer, combine beer, oil and yeast in large mixer bowl. Add 1 cup flour and salt; mix on low speed with paddle blade, adding enough flour to make soft dough that cleans the bowl. Change to dough hook and knead on medium-low speed, adding more flour if needed, 8 minutes or until dough is soft, smooth and elastic.

BEER-BRINED GRILLED PORK CHOPS
MAKES 4 SERVINGS

1 bottle (12 ounces) dark beer

¼ cup packed dark brown sugar

1 tablespoon salt

1 tablespoon chili powder

2 cloves garlic, minced

3 cups ice water

4 pork chops (1 inch thick)

Grilled Rosemary Potatoes (recipe follows)

1 Whisk beer, brown sugar, salt, chili powder and garlic in medium bowl until salt is dissolved. Add ice water and stir until ice melts. Add pork chops; place medium plate on top to keep chops submerged in brine. Refrigerate 3 to 4 hours.

2 Prepare grill for direct cooking over medium heat. Drain pork chops and pat dry with paper towels. Prepare Grilled Rosemary Potatoes. Grill pork chops, covered, 10 to 12 minutes. Serve with potatoes.

GRILLED ROSEMARY POTATOES

Place 4 quartered potatoes, ¼ cup chopped onion, 2 teaspoons chopped fresh rosemary and 1 teaspoon red pepper flakes on a 13×9-inch piece of foil. Toss mixture on foil; top with an additional 13×9-inch piece of foil. Seal edges of foil pieces together to make a packet. Grill 12 to 15 minutes or until potatoes are tender. Makes 4 servings.

TIP: Brining adds flavor and moisture to meats. Be sure that your pork chops have not been injected with a sodium solution (check the package label) or they could end up too salty.

PUB-STYLE FISH & CHIPS

MAKES 4 SERVINGS

¾ **cup all-purpose flour, plus additional for dusting fish**

½ **cup flat beer**

Vegetable oil

3 **large or 4 medium russet potatoes**

1 **egg, separated**

Salt

1 **pound cod fillets**

Prepared tartar sauce

Lemon wedges

1 Combine ¾ cup flour, beer and 2 teaspoons oil in small bowl; mix well. Cover and refrigerate 30 minutes to 2 hours.

2 Peel potatoes and cut into ¾-inch sticks. Place in large bowl of cold water. Pour at least 2 inches of oil into deep heavy saucepan or deep fryer; heat over medium heat to 320°F. Drain and thoroughly dry potatoes. Fry in batches 3 minutes or until slightly softened but not browned. Drain on paper towel-lined plate.

3 Stir egg yolk into cold flour mixture. Beat egg white in medium bowl with electric mixer at medium-high speed until soft peaks form. Fold egg white into flour mixture. Season batter with pinch of salt.

4 Preheat oven to 200°F. Heat oil in large saucepan to 365°F. Cut fish into pieces about 6 inches long and 2 to 3 inches wide; remove any pin bones. Dust fish with flour; dip fish into batter, shaking off excess. Lower carefully into oil; cook in batches 4 to 6 minutes or until batter is browned and fish is cooked through, turning once. (Allow temperature of oil to return to 365°F between batches.) Drain on paper towel-lined plate; keep warm in oven.

5 Return potatoes to hot oil; cook in batches 5 minutes or until browned and crisp. Drain on paper towel-lined plate; sprinkle with salt. Serve fish with potatoes, tartar sauce and lemon wedges.

BEEFY TOSTADA PIE

MAKES 4 TO 5 SERVINGS

2 teaspoons olive oil

1½ cups chopped onion

2 pounds ground beef

1 teaspoon chili powder

1 teaspoon ground cumin

1 teaspoon salt

2 cloves garlic, minced

1 can (15 ounces) tomato sauce

1 cup sliced black olives

8 flour tortillas

4 cups (16 ounces) shredded Cheddar cheese

Sour cream, salsa and chopped green onion (optional)

SLOW COOKER DIRECTIONS

1 Heat oil in large skillet over medium heat. Add onion and cook until tender. Add ground beef, chili powder, cumin, salt and garlic; cook until browned. Stir in tomato sauce; heat through. Stir in black olives.

2 Make foil handles using three 18×2-inch strips of heavy-duty foil. Crisscross foil to form spoke design. Place in slow cooker. Lay one tortilla on foil strips. Spread with meat sauce and layer of cheese. Top with another tortilla, meat sauce and cheese. Repeat layers ending with cheese. Cover; cook on HIGH 1½ hours.

3 To serve, lift out of slow cooker using foil handles and transfer to serving platter. Discard foil. Cut into wedges. Serve with sour cream, salsa and chopped green onion, if desired.

SMOKED TURKEY BREAST WITH CHIPOTLE RUB

MAKES 8 TO 10 SERVINGS

Mesquite or hickory wood chips

2 tablespoons packed dark brown sugar

2 tablespoons ground cumin

1 tablespoon salt

1 tablespoon garlic powder

1 tablespoon smoked paprika

2 teaspoons ground red pepper

1 teaspoon chili powder

¼ cup light butter-and-oil spread

1 (5½- to 6-pound) bone-in skin-on turkey breast

1 Prepare grill for indirect cooking over medium-high heat. Soak wood chips in water at least 30 minutes.

2 Combine brown sugar, cumin, salt, garlic powder, paprika, red pepper and chili powder in small bowl; mix well. Place 2 tablespoons spice mixture in another small bowl. Add butter spread; mix well.

3 Gently loosen skin of turkey breast. Spread butter mixture under skin onto breast. Rub skin and cavity of turkey with remaining spice mixture.

4 Remove some wood chips from water. Place chips in small foil tray. Place tray under grill grid directly on the heat source; allow wood to begin to smolder, about 10 minutes.

5 Grill turkey, covered, 1 hour. Replenish wood chips after 1 hour. Grill until cooked through (165°F). Remove to cutting board. Let stand 10 minutes before slicing.

CHICKEN AND MUSHROOM FETTUCCINE ALFREDO

MAKES 6 TO 8 SERVINGS

1½ pounds chicken breast tenders

2 packages (8 ounces each) cremini mushrooms, cut into thirds

½ teaspoon salt

¼ teaspoon black pepper

¼ teaspoon garlic powder

2 packages (8 ounces each) cream cheese, cut into chunks

1½ cups grated Parmesan cheese, plus additional for garnish

1½ cups whole milk

1 cup (2 sticks) butter, cut into pieces

1 package (1 pound) fettuccine

Chopped fresh Italian parsley

SLOW COOKER DIRECTIONS

1 Lightly coat 5-quart slow cooker with nonstick cooking spray. Arrange chicken in single layer in bottom of slow cooker. Top with mushrooms; sprinkle with salt, pepper and garlic powder.

2 Combine cream cheese, 1½ cups Parmesan cheese, milk and butter in medium saucepan over medium heat. Whisk constantly until smooth and heated through. Pour over mushrooms, pushing down any that float to surface. Cover; cook on LOW 4 to 5 hours or on HIGH 2 to 2½ hours.

3 Cook fettuccine according to package directions; drain. Add to slow cooker; toss to coat. Garnish with additional Parmesan cheese and parsley.

SESAME HOISIN BEER-CAN CHICKEN

MAKES 8 TO 10 SERVINGS

- 1 can (12 ounces) beer, divided
- ½ cup hoisin sauce
- 2 tablespoons honey
- 1 tablespoon soy sauce
- 1 teaspoon chili garlic sauce
- ½ teaspoon dark sesame oil
- 1 whole chicken (3½ to 4 pounds)

1 Prepare grill for indirect cooking over medium heat. Combine 2 tablespoons beer, hoisin sauce, honey, soy sauce, chili garlic sauce and oil in small bowl. Gently loosen skin of chicken over breast meat, legs and thighs. Spoon half of hoisin mixture evenly under skin and into cavity. Pour off beer until can is two-thirds full. Hold chicken upright with opening of cavity pointing down. Insert beer can into cavity.

2 Oil grill grid. Stand chicken upright on can over drip pan. Spread legs slightly to help support chicken. Cover; grill 30 minutes. Brush chicken with remaining hoisin mixture. Cover; grill 45 to 60 minutes or until chicken is cooked through (165°F). Use metal tongs to remove chicken and can to cutting board; let rest, standing up, 5 minutes. Carefully remove can and discard. Carve chicken and serve.

JAMBALAYA

MAKES 6 TO 8 SERVINGS

- 1 package (16 ounces) Cajun sausage, sliced
- 1 cup chopped onion
- 1 cup chopped green bell pepper
- 2 cloves garlic, minced
- 2 cups uncooked rice
- 2 cups chicken broth
- 1 bottle (12 ounces) light-colored beer, such as pale ale
- 1 can (about 14 ounces) diced tomatoes with green pepper, onion and celery
- 1 teaspoon Cajun seasoning
- 1 pound medium cooked shrimp, peeled and deveined (with tails on)

  Chopped fresh parsley (optional)

  Hot pepper sauce (optional)

1 Brown sausage in large Dutch oven over medium-high heat; drain fat. Add onion, bell pepper and garlic; cook and stir 2 to 3 minutes or until tender. Add rice, broth and beer. Cover; bring to a boil. Reduce heat to low. Simmer 20 minutes, stirring occasionally.

2 Stir in tomatoes and Cajun seasoning; cook 5 minutes. Add shrimp; cook 2 to 3 minutes or until heated through. Sprinkle with parsley and hot pepper sauce, if desired.

TEX-MEX BEEF WRAPS

MAKES 6 SERVINGS

- 1 tablespoon chili powder
- 2 teaspoons ground cumin
- 1 teaspoon salt
- ¼ teaspoon ground red pepper, or to taste
- 1 boneless beef chuck pot roast (2½ to 3 pounds), cut into 4 pieces
- 1 medium onion, chopped
- 3 cloves garlic, minced
- 1 cup salsa, divided
- 12 (6- to 7-inch) flour or corn tortillas, warmed
- 1 cup (4 ounces) shredded Cheddar or Monterey Jack cheese
- 1 cup chopped tomato
- 1 ripe avocado, diced
- ¼ cup chopped fresh cilantro

SLOW COOKER DIRECTIONS

1 Blend chili powder, cumin, salt and red pepper in small bowl. Rub mixture on all surfaces of meat.

2 Place onion and garlic in 4-quart slow cooker; top with meat. Spoon ½ cup salsa over meat. Cover; cook on LOW 8 to 9 hours or on HIGH 3½ to 4½ hours.

3 Remove meat to large cutting board. Shred meat with 2 forks. Skim off and discard fat from juices in slow cooker; return meat to juices and mix well. Adjust seasonings. Place meat mixture on warm tortillas; top with cheese, tomato, avocado and cilantro. Roll up to enclose filling. Serve with remaining salsa.

GRILLED CHICKEN WITH CORN AND BLACK BEAN SALSA

MAKES 4 SERVINGS

½ cup corn

½ cup finely chopped red bell pepper

½ of a 15-ounce can black beans, rinsed and drained

½ ripe medium avocado, diced

¼ cup chopped fresh cilantro

2 tablespoons fresh lime juice

1 tablespoon chopped pickled jalapeño pepper

½ teaspoon salt, divided

1 teaspoon black pepper

½ teaspoon chili powder

4 boneless skinless chicken breasts (4 ounces each), pounded to ½-inch thickness

1 Combine corn, bell pepper, beans, avocado, cilantro, lime juice, jalapeño pepper and ¼ teaspoon salt in medium bowl. Set aside.

2 Combine black pepper, remaining ¼ teaspoon salt and chili powder in small bowl; sprinkle over chicken.

3 Coat grill pan with nonstick cooking spray. Cook chicken over medium-high heat 4 minutes per side or until no longer pink in center.

4 Serve chicken topped with salsa.

CRISPY BUTTERMILK FRIED CHICKEN

MAKES 4 SERVINGS

- 2 cups buttermilk
- 1 tablespoon hot pepper sauce
- 3 pounds bone-in chicken pieces
- 2 cups all-purpose flour
- 2 teaspoons salt
- 2 teaspoons poultry seasoning
- 1 teaspoon garlic salt
- 1 teaspoon paprika
- 1 teaspoon ground red pepper
- 1 teaspoon black pepper
- 1 cup vegetable oil

1 Combine buttermilk and hot pepper sauce in large resealable food storage bag. Add chicken; seal bag. Turn to coat. Refrigerate 2 hours or up to 24 hours.

2 Combine flour, salt, poultry seasoning, garlic salt, paprika, red pepper and black pepper in another large resealable food storage bag or shallow baking dish; mix well. Working in batches, remove chicken from buttermilk; shake off excess. Add to flour mixture; shake to coat.

3 Heat oil over medium heat in heavy deep skillet until deep-fry thermometer registers 350°F. Working in batches, fry chicken 30 minutes or until cooked through (165°F), turning occasionally to brown all sides. Drain on paper towels.

NOTE

Carefully monitor the temperature of the oil during cooking. It should not drop below 325°F or go higher than 350°F. The chicken can also be cooked in a deep fryer following the manufacturer's directions. Never leave hot oil unattended.

QUICK CHICKEN QUESADILLAS

MAKES 4 SERVINGS

- 4 boneless skinless chicken breasts
- 3 tablespoons vegetable oil, divided
- ½ teaspoon salt
- 1 large yellow onion, thinly sliced
- 8 (6- to 8-inch) flour tortillas
- 3 cups (12 ounces) shredded mild Cheddar or Monterey Jack cheese
- Salsa, sour cream and/or guacamole (optional)

1 Flatten chicken breasts and cut into 1×¼-inch strips.

2 Heat 2 tablespoons oil in large skillet. Add chicken and cook, stirring over high heat, 3 to 4 minutes or until lightly browned and cooked through. Season with salt. Remove to plate.

3 Add onion to skillet; cook and stir about 5 minutes or until translucent. Remove to plate.

4 Heat remaining 1 tablespoon oil in same skillet. Place 1 tortilla in skillet; top with one quarter of chicken, onion and cheese. Place second tortilla over filling; press down lightly. Cook quesadilla about 2 minutes per side or until browned and crisp. Repeat with remaining tortillas and filling.

5 Cut into wedges; serve with desired toppings.

NOTE

Be creative and use your own favorite fillings!

TANGY BARBECUED LAMB

MAKES 6 SERVINGS

¾ cup chili sauce

½ cup beer (not light beer)

½ cup honey

¼ cup reduced-sodium Worcestershire sauce

¼ cup finely chopped onion

2 cloves garlic, minced

½ teaspoon red pepper flakes

¼ teaspoon sea salt

5 pounds lamb ribs, well trimmed and cut into individual ribs

1 Combine chili sauce, beer, honey, Worcestershire sauce, onion, garlic, red pepper flakes and salt in small saucepan; bring to a boil. Reduce heat; simmer, covered, 10 minutes. Remove from heat; cool to room temperature.

2 Place lamb in large resealable food storage bag; add chili mixture. Seal bag tightly; turn to coat. Marinate in refrigerator at least 2 hours, turning occasionally.

3 Prepare grill for indirect cooking. Oil grid.

4 Remove lamb from marinade; reserve marinade. Arrange lamb on grid over drip pan. Grill, covered, over medium heat 45 minutes or until lamb is tender, turning and brushing with marinade every 15 minutes. Place remaining marinade in small saucepan and bring to a boil; boil 1 minute. Serve with lamb.

NOTE

To set up gas grill for indirect cooking, preheat all burners on high. Turn one burner off; place food over "off" burner. Reset remaining burner(s) to medium. Close lid to cook. To set up charcoal grill for indirect cooking, arrange hot coals around outer edge of grill; place disposable foil pan in open space. Place food over open area, and close lid to cook.

SPICY POTATOES WITH TRI-TIP ROAST

MAKES 8 SERVINGS

- 4 teaspoons chili powder
- 2 teaspoons dried oregano
- ½ teaspoon salt
- 3 pounds unpeeled round red potatoes (about 9 potatoes)
- 3 tablespoons lime juice, divided
- 1 tablespoon olive oil
- 1 boneless lean beef loin tri-tip roast (about 1¾ pounds)

1 Preheat oven to 455°F. For seasoning mix, combine chili powder, oregano and salt in small bowl; set aside. Lightly coat 13×9-inch baking dish with nonstick cooking spray; set aside.

2 Cut potatoes into wedges. Toss potatoes with 2 tablespoons lime juice, oil and 1 tablespoon seasoning mix in large bowl. Spread in single layer in prepared baking dish.

3 Brush beef roast with remaining 1 tablespoon lime juice. Rub with remaining spice mixture. Place beef roast on rack in roasting pan. Roast 10 minutes.

4 Place potatoes beside or below roast in oven. Continue roasting 40 to 50 minutes or until thermometer inserted into center of roast registers 150°F. Remove roast and potatoes from oven. Cover both loosely with foil. Let roast stand 10 minutes before carving. (Temperature of meat will rise about 10° during standing.)

5 Thinly slice roast across grain. Serve with potatoes.

CHIPOTLE STRIP STEAKS

MAKES 4 SERVINGS

- 1 tablespoon olive oil
- ⅓ cup finely chopped onion
- ¾ cup beer
- 1 teaspoon Worcestershire sauce
- ⅓ cup ketchup
- 1 tablespoon red wine vinegar
- 1 teaspoon sugar
- ⅛ to ¼ teaspoon chipotle chili powder
- 4 bone-in strip steaks (8 to 9 ounces each)
- 1 teaspoon salt

1 Heat oil in small saucepan over medium-high heat. Add onion; cook 3 minutes or until softened, stirring occasionally. Add beer and Worcestershire sauce; bring to a boil, stirring occasionally. Cook until reduced to about ⅓ cup. Stir in ketchup, vinegar, sugar and chipotle chili powder; simmer over medium-low heat 3 minutes or until thickened, stirring occasionally. Keep warm.

2 Prepare grill for direct cooking over medium-high heat. Spray grid with nonstick cooking spray. Sprinkle steaks with salt.

3 Grill steaks 4 to 5 minutes per side for medium rare (145°F) or until desired doneness. Serve with chipotle sauce.

GRILLED CHILI-MARINATED PORK

MAKES 6 TO 8 SERVINGS

- 3 tablespoons ground seeded dried pasilla chiles
- 1 teaspoon coarse or kosher salt
- ½ teaspoon ground cumin
- 2 tablespoons vegetable oil
- 1 tablespoon fresh lime juice
- 3 cloves garlic, minced
- 2 pounds pork tenderloin or thick boneless pork loin chops, trimmed of fat

   Shredded romaine lettuce (optional)

   Radishes (optional)

1 Mix chiles, salt and cumin in small bowl. Stir in oil and lime juice to make smooth paste. Stir in garlic.

2 Butterfly pork by cutting lengthwise about ⅔ of the way through, leaving meat in one piece; spread meat flat. Cut tenderloin crosswise into 8 equal pieces. If using pork chops, do not cut chops into pieces.

3 Place pork between pieces of plastic wrap. Pound with flat side of meat mallet to ¼-inch thickness.

4 Spread chili paste on both sides of pork pieces to coat evenly. Place in shallow glass baking dish. Marinate, covered, in refrigerator 2 to 3 hours.

5 Prepare coals for grill or preheat broiler. Grill or broil pork 6 inches from heat 8 to 10 minutes for grilling or 6 to 7 minutes for broiling, turning once. Serve on lettuce-lined plate. Garnish with radishes, if desired.

FLANK STEAK GRILL ➔
MAKES 6 TO 8 SERVINGS

½ cup vegetable oil

¼ cup soy sauce

2 tablespoons lemon juice

1 tablespoon minced garlic in olive oil

2 teaspoons dried thyme

1 beef flank steak (1½ to 2 pounds)

1 Combine oil, soy sauce, lemon juice, garlic and thyme in large resealable food bag. Add steak, turning to coat. Close bag; marinate in refrigerator 30 minutes to 3 hours.

2 Preheat grill for direct cooking. Spray grid with nonstick cooking spray.

3 Remove meat from marinade; discard marinade. Grill steak over medium heat, uncovered, 17 to 21 minutes for medium rare (145°F) or until desired doneness, turning once. Remove steak from grill. Lightly cover with foil; let stand 15 minutes. Thinly slice steak across the grain.

SUPER-EASY BEEF BURRITOS
MAKES 4 SERVINGS

1 boneless beef chuck roast (2 to 3 pounds)

1 can (28 ounces) enchilada sauce

Water (optional)

4 (8-inch) flour tortillas

SLOW COOKER DIRECTIONS

1 Place roast in slow cooker; cover with enchilada sauce. Add 2 to 3 tablespoons water, if desired.

2 Cover; cook on LOW 6 to 8 hours or until beef begins to fall apart. Shred beef; serve in tortillas.

FAMILY-STYLE BEEF PIZZA
MAKES 6 SERVINGS

- 1 package (about 14 ounces) refrigerated pizza dough
- ¼ pound 95% lean ground beef
- 3 tablespoons finely chopped onion
- ¾ cup pizza sauce
- 1 small tomato, peeled, seeded and chopped
- 2 teaspoons Italian seasoning
- 2 cloves garlic, minced
- ⅛ teaspoon ground red pepper
- ½ cup sliced mushrooms
- 1 cup (4 ounces) shredded part-skim mozzarella cheese
- 1 tablespoon finely grated Parmesan cheese

1 Preheat oven to 425°F. Lightly spray 12-inch pizza pan with nonstick cooking spray. Unroll pizza dough; press onto prepared pan, making slight edge around rim. Prick dough all over with fork. Bake 7 to 10 minutes or until lightly browned.

2 Meanwhile, brown ground beef with onion in large skillet over medium-high heat 6 to 8 minutes, stirring to break up meat. Drain fat.

3 Combine pizza sauce, tomato, Italian seasoning, garlic and red pepper in small saucepan over medium heat; bring to a boil. Reduce heat; simmer, uncovered, about 8 minutes or until desired consistency.

4 Spread sauce evenly over pizza crust. Sprinkle with ground beef mixture and mushrooms. Sprinkle with cheeses. Bake 5 to 8 minutes or until heated through.

MESQUITE-GRILLED CHICKEN QUARTERS

MAKES 8 SERVINGS

- 2 whole chickens (about 3½ pounds each), cut into quarters
- 2 tablespoons vegetable oil
- 1 small onion, chopped
- 1 clove garlic, minced
- 1 can (12 ounces) beer
- ½ cup tomato juice
- ½ cup ketchup
- ¼ cup Worcestershire sauce
- 2 tablespoons packed brown sugar
- 1 tablespoon lemon juice
- 2 teaspoons chili powder
- 1 teaspoon dry mustard
- ¼ teaspoon salt
- ¼ teaspoon black pepper

1 Preheat oven to 350°F. Place chickens in 1 large or 2 medium baking pans; cover tightly with foil. Bake 30 minutes. Remove from oven; uncover. Cool.

2 Heat oil in 2-quart saucepan over medium heat. Add onion and garlic; cook until onion is tender. Whisk beer, tomato juice, ketchup, Worcestershire sauce, brown sugar, lemon juice, chili powder, dry mustard, salt and pepper into saucepan until well blended. Bring to a boil. Reduce heat and simmer, stirring occasionally, 20 minutes or until sauce is thickened slightly and is reduced to about 2 cups. Let cool.

3 Place chickens into 2 large resealable food storage bags. Dividing marinade equally, pour over chicken in each bag; seal bags. Refrigerate 8 hours or overnight.

4 Preheat grill for direct cooking. Remove chickens from marinade and drain well. Reserve marinade. Hook wing tips back behind body joint on breast pieces of chicken. Grill leg and thigh quarters on hottest part of grill 4 to 6 inches above heat; grill breast pieces on cooler edges of grill. Cook, turning occasionally, 20 to 25 minutes or until cooked through (165°F).

5 Meanwhile, place marinade in small saucepan; bring to a boil over medium-high heat. Boil 2 minutes; remove from heat and cool. Brush chicken generously with marinade during last 10 minutes of cooking.

KOREAN BEEF SHORT RIBS

MAKES 4 TO 6 SERVINGS

2½ pounds beef chuck flanken-style short ribs, cut ⅜ to ½ inch thick*

¼ cup chopped green onions

¼ cup water

¼ cup soy sauce

1 tablespoon sugar

2 teaspoons grated fresh ginger

2 teaspoons dark sesame oil

2 cloves garlic, minced

½ teaspoon black pepper

1 tablespoon sesame seeds, toasted

Flanken-style ribs can be ordered from your butcher. They are cross-cut short ribs sawed through the bones.

1 Place ribs in large resealable food storage bag. Combine green onions, water, soy sauce, sugar, ginger, oil, garlic and pepper in small bowl; pour over ribs. Seal bag; turn to coat. Marinate in refrigerator at least 4 hours or up to 8 hours, turning occasionally.

2 Prepare grill for direct cooking. Remove ribs from marinade; reserve marinade. Grill ribs, covered, over medium-high heat 5 minutes. Brush lightly with reserved marinade; turn and brush again. Discard remaining marinade. Continue to grill, covered, 5 to 6 minutes for medium (160°F) or to desired doneness. Sprinkle with sesame seeds.

BEER OVEN-FRIED CHICKEN

MAKES 4 SERVINGS

- 1⅓ cups light-colored beer, such as pale ale
- 2 tablespoons buttermilk
- 1¼ cups panko bread crumbs*
- ½ cup grated Parmesan cheese
- 4 chicken breast cutlets (about 1¼ pounds)
- ½ teaspoon salt
- ¼ teaspoon black pepper

Panko bread crumbs are Japanese bread crumbs that are much lighter and less dense than ones often used in America. Panko bread crumbs can be found in Asian markets or in the Asian foods section of your supermarket.

1. Preheat oven to 400°F. Line large baking sheet with foil.

2. Combine beer and buttermilk in shallow bowl. Combine panko and cheese in another shallow bowl.

3. Sprinkle chicken with salt and pepper. Dip in beer mixture; roll in panko mixture to coat. Place on prepared baking sheet.

4. Bake 25 to 30 minutes or until chicken is no longer pink in center.

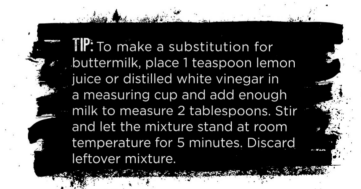

TIP: To make a substitution for buttermilk, place 1 teaspoon lemon juice or distilled white vinegar in a measuring cup and add enough milk to measure 2 tablespoons. Stir and let the mixture stand at room temperature for 5 minutes. Discard leftover mixture.

KICK ASS SIDES

CHILI CHEESE FRIES

MAKES 4 SERVINGS

1½ pounds ground beef

1 medium onion, chopped

2 cloves garlic, minced

½ cup lager

2 tablespoons chili powder

2 tablespoons tomato paste

Salt and black pepper

1 package (32 ounces) frozen French fries

1 jar (15 ounces) cheese sauce, heated

Sour cream and chopped green onions (optional)

1 Brown beef, onion and garlic in large skillet over medium-high heat 6 to 8 minutes, stirring to break up meat. Drain fat.

2 Stir lager, chili powder and tomato paste into beef mixture. Simmer, stirring occasionally, 20 minutes or until most liquid has evaporated. Season with salt and pepper.

3 Meanwhile, bake French fries according to package directions.

4 Divide French fries evenly among bowls. Top evenly with chili and cheese sauce. Garnish with sour cream and green onions.

GRILLED POTATO SALAD

MAKES 4 SERVINGS

¼ cup country-style Dijon mustard

2 tablespoons chopped fresh dill

1 tablespoon white wine vinegar or cider vinegar

1½ teaspoons salt, divided

¼ teaspoon black pepper

5 tablespoons olive oil, divided

8 cups water

2 pounds small red potatoes

1 green onion, thinly sliced

1 Prepare grill for direct cooking.

2 Whisk mustard, dill, vinegar, ½ teaspoon salt and pepper in measuring cup. Gradually whisk in 3 tablespoons oil. Set aside.

3 Bring water and remaining 1 teaspoon salt to a boil in large saucepan over medium-high heat. Cut potatoes into ½-inch slices. Add potatoes to saucepan; boil 5 minutes. Drain; return potatoes to saucepan. Drizzle with remaining 2 tablespoons oil; toss lightly.

4 Spray one side of large foil sheet with nonstick cooking spray. Transfer potatoes to foil; fold into packet. Place potato packet on grid. Grill 10 minutes or until potatoes are tender. Transfer potatoes to serving bowl. Sprinkle with green onion. Add dressing and toss gently to coat. Serve warm.

ONION RING STACK

MAKES 4 TO 6 SERVINGS (ABOUT 20 ONION RINGS)

1 cup all-purpose flour, divided

½ cup cornmeal

1 teaspoon black pepper

½ teaspoon salt

¼ to ½ teaspoon ground red pepper

1 cup light-colored beer

Rémoulade Sauce (recipe follows) or ranch dressing

Vegetable oil for frying

6 tablespoons cornstarch, divided

2 large sweet onions, cut into ½-inch rings and separated

1 Combine ½ cup flour, cornmeal, black pepper, salt and red pepper in large bowl; mix well. Whisk in beer until well blended. Let stand 1 hour.

2 Prepare Rémoulade Sauce; refrigerate until ready to serve.

3 Pour oil into large saucepan or Dutch oven to depth of 2 inches; heat to 360° to 370°F. Line large wire rack with paper towels.

4 Whisk 4 tablespoons cornstarch into batter. Combine remaining ½ cup flour and 2 tablespoons cornstarch in medium bowl. Thoroughly coat onions with flour mixture.

5 Working with one at a time, dip onion rings into batter to coat completely; carefully place in hot oil. Cook about 4 onions rings at a time 3 minutes or until golden brown, turning once. Remove to prepared wire rack; season with additional salt. Return oil to 370°F between batches. Serve immediately with Remoulade Sauce.

RÉMOULADE SAUCE

Combine 1 cup mayonnaise, 2 tablespoons coarse-grain mustard, 1 tablespoon lemon juice, 1 tablespoon sweet relish, 1 teaspoon horseradish sauce, 1 teaspoon Worcestershire sauce and ¼ teaspoon hot pepper sauce in medium bowl; mix well.

SPICY GRILLED CORN ➡

MAKES 4 SERVINGS

- 2 tablespoons butter, softened
- 1 tablespoon chopped fresh parsley
- 2 teaspoons lemon juice
- ½ teaspoon salt
- ½ teaspoon black pepper
- ½ teaspoon red pepper flakes
- 4 ears corn, husks and silks removed

1 Prepare grill for direct cooking. Combine butter, parsley, lemon juice, salt, black pepper and red pepper flakes in small bowl. Brush mixture evenly over corn.

2 Place 2 sheets of foil (about 12×18 inches each) on work surface; center 2 ears of corn on each piece of foil. Bring up sides of foil; fold over top and edges to seal packets.

3 Grill packets over medium-high heat, covered, about 15 minutes or until corn is tender, turning once.

HICKORY-FLAVORED BAKED BEANS

MAKES 6 SERVINGS

- 4 slices bacon, cut into ½-inch pieces
- ½ cup chopped onion
- 1 can (28 ounces) baked beans
- ½ cup hickory-flavored barbecue sauce
- 2 tablespoons packed brown sugar
- 1 teaspoon dry mustard
- ¼ teaspoon hot pepper sauce (optional)

Preheat oven to 350°F. In large ovenproof skillet, cook bacon and onion over medium-high heat until bacon is browned and crisp; drain fat. Add remaining ingredients; mix well. Bake, uncovered, 30 minutes or until hot and bubbly.

SERVING SUGGESTION

Serve with simple picnic foods like hot dogs or fancier fare such as grilled chicken or pork chops.

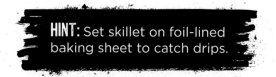

HINT: Set skillet on foil-lined baking sheet to catch drips.

CHEESY GARLIC BREAD
MAKES 8 TO 10 SERVINGS

1 loaf (about 16 ounces) Italian bread

½ cup (1 stick) butter, softened

8 cloves garlic, very thinly sliced

¼ cup grated Parmesan cheese

2 cups (8 ounces) shredded mozzarella cheese

1 Preheat oven to 425°F. Line large baking sheet with foil.

2 Cut bread in half horizontally. Spread cut sides of bread evenly with butter; top with sliced garlic. Sprinkle with Parmesan, then mozzarella cheeses. Place on prepared baking sheet.

3 Bake 12 minutes or until cheeses are melted and golden brown in spots. Cut crosswise into slices. Serve warm.

BACON-ROASTED BRUSSELS SPROUTS ❯

MAKES 4 SERVINGS

1 pound Brussels sprouts

3 slices bacon, cut into ½-inch pieces

2 teaspoons packed brown sugar

Salt and black pepper

1 Preheat oven to 400°F. Trim ends from Brussels sprouts; cut in half lengthwise.

2 Combine Brussels sprouts, bacon and brown sugar in glass baking dish.

3 Roast 25 to 30 minutes or until golden brown, stirring once. Season with salt and pepper.

SPICY BLACK-EYED PEAS AND RICE

MAKES 6 SERVINGS

1 tablespoon canola oil

½ cup minced onions

1 clove garlic, minced

1½ cups water

2 cups frozen black-eyed peas (no-salt-added)

¼ cup diced tomatoes with green chiles or jalapeños, drained

1 teaspoon black pepper

1⅓ cups cooked brown rice

1 Heat oil in 3-quart saucepan over medium heat; add onions and cook 4 minutes or until beginning to turn light golden color, stirring often. Add garlic, cook 15 seconds.

2 Add water, black-eyed peas, tomatoes and pepper to onion mixture; stir and bring to a boil over high heat. Reduce heat to a simmer; cover and cook 18 to 20 minutes or until tender.

3 Use slotted spoon to remove black-eyed peas. Reduce liquid by cooking on high 2 to 3 minutes. Add reduced liquid to black-eyed peas and stir. Serve peas over brown rice.

GRILLED ROMAINE HEARTS WITH TANGY VINAIGRETTE

MAKES 6 SERVINGS

TANGY VINAIGRETTE

- 3 cups cola beverage
- ⅓ cup white vinegar
- ⅓ cup canola oil
- ¼ cup sugar
- 1 teaspoon salt
- ½ teaspoon onion powder
- ½ teaspoon garlic powder
- 3 tablespoons ketchup
- 1 tablespoon balsamic vinegar
- ⅛ teaspoon black pepper
- 2 tablespoons honey mustard

ROMAINE HEARTS

- 6 romaine hearts
- ¼ to ½ cup olive oil
  Salt and black pepper

1 Combine cola, white vinegar, canola oil, sugar, 1 teaspoon salt, onion powder, garlic powder, ketchup, balsamic vinegar, ⅛ teaspoon pepper and mustard in medium bowl; set aside.

2 Prepare grill for direct cooking over medium-high heat. Cut romaine hearts in half lengthwise; drizzle with olive oil and sprinkle generously with salt and pepper.

3 Grill about 2 minutes per side or until wilted and lightly charred.

4 Drizzle with vinaigrette. Refrigerate remaining vinaigrette for another use.

KIELBASA, CABBAGE AND ONIONS

MAKES 6 SERVINGS

2 tablespoons olive oil

1 pound kielbasa, cut in half lengthwise then cut diagonally into ¾-inch slices

1 onion, thinly sliced

2 teaspoons fennel seeds

1 teaspoon caraway seeds

1 clove garlic, minced

½ cup water

1 pound cabbage (6 cups or ½ head), thinly sliced

2 pounds (5 medium) unpeeled red potatoes, cut into ¾-inch pieces

1 bottle (12 ounces) lager beer or ale

½ teaspoon salt

¼ teaspoon black pepper

1 Heat oil in large skillet over medium heat. Add kielbasa; cook 5 minutes or until browned. Remove to plate with slotted spoon.

2 Add onion, fennel seeds, caraway seeds and garlic to skillet; cook and stir 2 to 3 minutes or until onion is translucent. Add ½ cup water, scraping up browned bits from bottom of skillet. Add cabbage and potatoes; cook 10 minutes or until cabbage is wilted, stirring occasionally.

3 Stir in lager; cover and cook over medium-low heat 15 minutes or until potatoes are tender. Season with salt and pepper; cook over medium heat 15 minutes until beer has reduced to sauce consistency. Return kielbasa to skillet; cook until heated through.

PEPPERONI-OREGANO FOCACCIA

MAKES 12 SERVINGS

1 tablespoon cornmeal

1 package (about 14 ounces) refrigerated pizza dough

½ cup finely chopped pepperoni (about 3 ounces)

1½ teaspoons finely chopped fresh oregano *or* ½ teaspoon dried oregano

2 teaspoons olive oil

1 Preheat oven to 425°F. Spray baking sheet with nonstick cooking spray; sprinkle with cornmeal. Set aside.

2 Unroll dough onto lightly floured surface. Pat dough into 12×9-inch rectangle. Sprinkle half of pepperoni and half of oregano over one side of dough. Fold over dough, making 12×4½-inch rectangle.

3 Roll dough into 12×9-inch rectangle. Place on prepared baking sheet. Prick dough with fork at 2-inch intervals (about 30 times). Brush with oil; sprinkle with remaining pepperoni and oregano.

4 Bake 12 to 15 minutes or until golden brown. (Prick dough several more times if it puffs as it bakes.) Cut into strips.

PICANTE PINTOS AND RICE

MAKES 8 SERVINGS

2 cups dried pinto beans, rinsed and sorted

1 can (about 14 ounces) no-salt-added stewed tomatoes

1 cup coarsely chopped onion

¾ cup coarsely chopped green bell pepper

¼ cup sliced celery

4 cloves garlic, minced

½ small jalapeño pepper,* seeded and chopped

2 teaspoons dried oregano

2 teaspoons chili powder

½ teaspoon ground red pepper

2 cups chopped kale

3 cups hot cooked brown rice

Jalapeño peppers can sting and irritate the skin, so wear rubber gloves when handling peppers and do not touch your eyes.

1 Place beans in large saucepan; add water to cover beans by 2 inches. Bring to a boil over high heat; boil 2 minutes. Remove from heat; let stand, covered, 1 hour. Drain beans; discard water. Return beans to saucepan.

2 Add 2 cups water, tomatoes, onion, bell pepper, celery, garlic, jalapeño pepper, oregano, chili powder and red pepper to saucepan; bring to a boil over high heat. Reduce heat to low. Simmer, covered, about 1½ hours or until beans are tender, stirring occasionally.

3 Gently stir kale into bean mixture. Simmer, uncovered, 30 minutes. (Beans will be very tender.) Serve over rice.

HOT AND SPICY SPUDS

MAKES 4 SERVINGS

4 medium baking potatoes
1 cup chopped onion
½ cup chopped green bell pepper
2 cloves garlic, minced
1 teaspoon olive oil
1 can (about 15 ounces) kidney beans, rinsed and drained
1 can (about 14 ounces) tomatoes, cut up and undrained
1 can (4 ounces) diced mild green chiles
¼ cup chopped fresh cilantro or parsley
1 teaspoon ground cumin
1 teaspoon chili powder
¼ teaspoon ground red pepper
¼ cup sour cream
¼ cup (1 ounce) shredded Cheddar cheese

1 Preheat oven to 350°F. Scrub potatoes; pierce with fork. Bake 1¼ to 1½ hours or until tender.

2 Meanwhile, spray 2-quart saucepan with nonstick cooking spray; heat saucepan over medium heat. Cook and stir onion, bell pepper and garlic in oil until vegetables are tender. Stir in beans, tomatoes with juice, chiles, cilantro, cumin, chili powder and red pepper. Bring to a boil over high heat. Reduce heat to medium-low. Cover; simmer 8 minutes, stirring occasionally.

3 Gently roll potatoes to loosen pulp. Cut crisscross slit in each potato. Place potatoes on 4 plates. Press potato ends to open slits. Spoon bean mixture over potatoes. Top with sour cream and sprinkle with cheese.

MEXICAN RICE OLÉ

MAKES 4 SERVINGS

1 teaspoon vegetable oil

1 cup uncooked long grain rice

1 teaspoon salt

1 clove garlic, minced

1 can (about 14 ounces) chicken broth

1 can (10¾ ounces) condensed cream of chicken soup, undiluted

¾ cup sour cream

1 can (4 ounces) chopped mild green chiies, undrained

⅓ cup salsa

1 teaspoon ground cumin

1 cup (4 ounces) shredded Cheddar cheese

1 can (about 2 ounces) sliced black olives, drained

1 Preheat oven to 350°F. Spray 3-quart casserole with nonstick cooking spray.

2 Heat oil in large skillet over medium heat. Add rice, salt and garlic; cook and stir 2 to 3 minutes or until rice is well coated. Add enough water to broth to equal 2 cups. Pour into skillet; cook about 15 minutes or until rice is tender, stirring occasionally.

3 Remove skillet from heat and add soup, sour cream, chiles, salsa and cumin; mix well. Transfer to prepared casserole.

4 Bake 20 minutes. Top with cheese and olives; bake 5 to 10 minutes or until cheese is melted and casserole is heated through.

MRS. GRADY'S BEANS

MAKES 6 TO 8 SERVINGS

½ pound 90% lean
    ground beef

1 small onion, chopped

8 slices bacon,
    chopped

1 can (about
    15 ounces) pinto
    beans, rinsed and
    drained

1 can (about
    15 ounces) butter
    beans, rinsed and
    drained, reserve
    ¼ cup liquid

1 can (about
    15 ounces) kidney
    beans, rinsed and
    drained

¼ cup ketchup

2 tablespoons
    molasses

½ teaspoon dry
    mustard

½ cup granulated sugar

¼ cup packed brown
    sugar

SLOW COOKER DIRECTIONS

1 Brown ground beef, onion and bacon in medium
saucepan over high heat. Stir in beans and reserved
liquid; set aside.

2 Combine ketchup, molasses and dry mustard in
medium bowl. Mix in sugars. Stir ketchup mixture
into beef mixture; mix well. Transfer to slow cooker.
Cover; cook on LOW 2 to 3 hours or until heated
through.

JAMAICAN GRILLED SWEET POTATOES

MAKES 6 SERVINGS

- 2 **large sweet potatoes or yams (about 1½ pounds)**
- 3 **tablespoons packed brown sugar**
- 3 **tablespoons melted butter, divided**
- 1 **teaspoon ground ginger**
- 1 **tablespoon chopped fresh cilantro**
- 2 **teaspoons dark rum**

1 Pierce potatoes in several places with fork. Place on paper towel in microwave. Microwave on HIGH 5 to 6 minutes or until crisp-tender, rotating one-fourth turn halfway through cooking time. Let stand 10 minutes. Diagonally slice potatoes into ¾-inch slices.

2 Prepare grill for direct cooking. Combine brown sugar, 1 tablespoon butter and ginger in small bowl; mix well. Stir in cilantro and rum; set aside. Lightly brush one side of each potato slice with half of remaining melted butter.

3 Grill sweet potato slices, butter side down, on covered grill over medium heat 4 to 6 minutes or until grillmarked. Brush tops with remaining melted butter. Turn; grill 3 to 5 minutes or until grillmarked. To serve, spoon rum mixture equally over potato slices.

PINEAPPLE HAM FRIED RICE
MAKES 4 TO 6 SERVINGS

- 8 ounces cooked smoked ham steak
- 3 tablespoons vegetable oil, divided
- 2 tablespoons sliced almonds
- 1 small green bell pepper, cut into strips
- 2 green onions, coarsely chopped
- 4 cups cooked rice, cooled
- 1 can (8 ounces) pineapple chunks packed in juice, undrained
- 2 tablespoons raisins
- 2 to 3 tablespoons reduced-sodium soy sauce
- 1 tablespoon dark sesame oil

1 Cut ham into 2-inch strips; set aside.

2 Heat wok over medium-high heat 1 minute or until hot. Drizzle 1 tablespoon vegetable oil into wok and heat 30 seconds. Add almonds; stir-fry until golden brown. Remove from wok.

3 Add remaining 2 tablespoons vegetable oil to wok and heat 30 seconds. Add ham, bell pepper and green onions; stir-fry 2 minutes. Add rice, pineapple with juice and raisins; stir-fry until heated through.

4 Stir in soy sauce and sesame oil; stir-fry until well mixed. Transfer to serving bowl. Sprinkle with almonds just before serving.

HOT POTATO SALAD

MAKES 6 SERVINGS

- 4 slices turkey bacon
- 1 cup diced yellow onion (about 1 medium)
- 2 pounds medium potatoes, peeled and cubed
- 3 tablespoons all-purpose flour
- ⅓ teaspoon salt (optional)
- ¼ cup red wine vinegar
- ⅓ cup sugar
- 3 tablespoons mayonnaise
- ¼ cup diced green onions (optional)

1 Heat large nonstick skillet over medium-high heat. Cook turkey bacon; set aside on separate plate. Add yellow onion to skillet; cook until beginning to brown, stirring frequently. Remove from heat, crumble bacon; return to skillet with yellow onion.

2 Meanwhile, bring 4 cups of water to a boil in large saucepan over high heat. Add potatoes; return to a boil. Reduce heat, cover and simmer 5 to 6 minutes or until tender. Drain; add potatoes to skillet with yellow onion mixture.

3 Whisk together flour, salt, if desired, vinegar, sugar and mayonnaise in small bowl. Pour over potato mixture; mix well to combine. Serve warm; top with diced green onions, if desired.

POTATO, BEER AND CHEESE GRATIN

MAKES 8 SERVINGS

1 bottle (12 ounces) light-colored beer, such as pale ale

2 sprigs fresh thyme

1 bay leaf

½ cup whipping cream

1 tablespoon all-purpose flour

2 cloves garlic, minced

2 pounds potatoes (about 3 large), unpeeled and thinly sliced

1 teaspoon salt

1 teaspoon black pepper

2 cups (8 ounces) shredded Gruyère or Emmenthaler cheese

2 tablespoons chopped fresh chives (optional)

1 Bring beer, thyme and bay leaf to a boil in medium saucepan. Reduce heat to low. Simmer 5 minutes or until liquid reduces to ¾ cup, stirring occasionally. Remove and discard thyme and bay leaf. Let cool.

2 Combine cream, flour and garlic in small bowl; mix well. Stir into beer mixture.

3 Preheat oven to 375°F. Grease 13×9-inch baking dish. Arrange half of potato slices in bottom of prepared dish, overlapping slightly. Sprinkle with salt and pepper. Pour half of beer mixture over potatoes; sprinkle with half of cheese. Repeat layers.

4 Cover; bake 30 minutes. *Reduce oven temperature to 350°F.* Uncover; bake 30 minutes or until potatoes are tender and top is golden brown. Let stand 10 minutes before serving. Garnish with chives.

VARIATION

Adding 1 teaspoon of minced jalapeño peppers to the gratin adds extra spice and balances the taste of the beer. Add the jalapeño peppers with the cheese in step 3.

SPICY SWEET POTATO MUFFINS

MAKES 12 MUFFINS

⅓ cup plus
    2 tablespoons
    packed brown
    sugar, divided

2 teaspoons ground
    cinnamon, divided

1½ cups all-purpose
    flour

2 teaspoons baking
    powder

½ teaspoon baking
    soda

½ teaspoon salt

½ teaspoon ground
    allspice

1 cup mashed cooked
    or canned sweet
    potatoes

¾ cup low-fat
    buttermilk

¼ cup vegetable oil

1 egg

1 Preheat oven to 425°F. Spray 12 standard (2½-inch) muffin cups with nonstick cooking spray. Combine 2 tablespoons brown sugar and 1 teaspoon cinnamon in small bowl; mix well.

2 Combine flour, remaining ⅓ cup brown sugar, 1 teaspoon cinnamon, baking powder, baking soda, salt and allspice in large bowl. Combine sweet potatoes, buttermilk, oil and egg in medium bowl; mix well. Stir into flour mixture just until moistened. Spoon evenly into prepared muffin cups. Sprinkle with brown sugar-cinnamon mixture.

3 Bake 14 to 16 minutes or until toothpick inserted into centers comes out clean. Remove to wire rack; cool completely.

DAMN GOOD DESSERTS

CHOCOLATE-COVERED BACON

MAKES 12 SLICES

12 slices thick-cut bacon

12 wooden skewers (12 inches)

1 cup semisweet chocolate chips

2 tablespoons shortening, divided

1 cup white chocolate chips or butterscotch chips

1 Thread each bacon slice onto wooden skewer. Place on rack in large baking pan. Bake at 400°F 20 to 25 minutes or until crisp. Cool completely.

2 Combine semisweet chocolate chips and 1 tablespoon shortening in large microwavable bowl. Microwave on HIGH at 30-second intervals until melted and smooth.

3 Combine white chocolate chips or butterscotch chips and remaining 1 tablespoon shortening in large microwavable bowl. Microwave on HIGH at 30-second intervals until melted and smooth.

4 Drizzle chocolates over each bacon slice as desired. Place on waxed paper-lined baking sheets. Refrigerate until firm. Store in refrigerator.

CHOCOLATE CAKE MILKSHAKE

MAKES 1 SERVING (2 CUPS)

1 slice (⅛ of cake) Rich Chocolate Cake (recipe follows)

½ cup milk

2 scoops vanilla ice cream (about 1 cup total)

1 Prepare and frost Rich Chocolate Cake.

2 Combine milk, ice cream and cake slice in blender; blend just until cake is incorporated but texture of shake is not completely smooth.

RICH CHOCOLATE CAKE

MAKES 8 TO 10 SERVINGS

1 package (about 15 ounces) devil's food cake mix

1 cup cold water

1 cup mayonnaise

3 eggs

1½ containers (16 ounces each) chocolate frosting

1 Preheat oven to 350°F. Spray 2 (9-inch) round cake pans with nonstick cooking spray.

2 Beat cake mix, water, mayonnaise and eggs in large bowl with electric mixer at low speed 30 seconds. Beat at medium speed 2 minutes. Pour into prepared pans.

3 Bake about 25 minutes or until toothpick inserted into centers comes out clean. Cool in pans 10 minutes; remove to wire racks to cool completely.

4 Fill and frost cake with chocolate frosting.

ICE CREAM PIZZA TREAT

MAKES 8 SERVINGS

24 chocolate sandwich cookies

1 jar (about 12 ounces) hot fudge ice cream topping, divided

2 pints vanilla ice cream

⅓ cup candy-coated chocolate pieces

1 Place cookies in food processor; pulse until large crumbs form. (Do not overprocess into fine crumbs.) Add ½ cup hot fudge topping; pulse just until blended. (Mixture should not be smooth; small cookie pieces may remain.)

2 Transfer mixture to pizza pan; press into even 11- to 12-inch layer about ¼ inch thick. Freeze crust 10 minutes. Meanwhile, remove ice cream from freezer to soften 10 minutes.

3 Spread ice cream evenly over crust (about ½-inch-thick layer), leaving ½-inch border. Return to freezer; freeze 2 hours or until firm.

4 Heat remaining hot fudge topping according to package directions. Drizzle over ice cream; top with chocolate pieces. Freeze 1 hour or until firm. Cut into wedges to serve.

S'MORE BANANAS
MAKES 8 SERVINGS

8 bananas

24 miniature
marshmallows

8 tablespoons mini
chocolate chips

8 tablespoons graham
cracker crumbs

1 Slice bananas lengthwise halfway through peel and flesh. Place each banana on 8×3-inch piece of foil. Place 3 marshmallows, 1 tablespoon chocolate chips and 1 tablespoon graham cracker crumbs in each banana slit. Roll up and seal foil around each banana.

2 Prepare grill for direct grilling. Grill wrapped bananas over medium heat 8 to 10 minutes or until soft. Carefully remove from grill; let cool before handling.

CHOCOLATE-PEANUT BUTTER BANANAS

Substitute chocolate syrup, peanut butter and peanuts for the marshmallows, chocolate chips and graham cracker crumbs. Cook as directed above. Makes 8 servings.

ICE CREAM SANDWICHES

MAKES 8 SANDWICHES

Candied Bacon (recipe follows), crumbled

1 package (about 18 ounces) chocolate cake mix with pudding in the mix

2 eggs

¼ cup warm water

3 tablespoons butter, melted

2 cups vanilla ice cream, softened

1 Prepare Candied Bacon.

2 Preheat oven to 350°F. Line 13×9-inch baking pan with foil; spray foil with nonstick cooking spray.

3 Beat cake mix, eggs, water and butter in large bowl with electric mixer until well blended. (Dough will be thick and sticky.) Press dough evenly into prepared pan; prick surface evenly with fork (about 40 times).

4 Bake 20 minutes or until toothpick inserted into center comes out clean. Cool in pan on wire rack.

5 Cut cookie in half crosswise; remove one half from pan. Spread ice cream evenly over cookie half remaining in pan. Top with second half.

6 Freeze at least 4 hours. Cut into 8 equal pieces; dip sides in Candied Bacon. Wrap sandwiches in parchment paper; freeze until ready to serve.

NOTE

If the ice cream is too hard to scoop easily, microwave on HIGH 10 seconds to soften.

CANDIED BACON

8 to 10 slices bacon

¼ to ½ cup packed brown sugar

Preheat oven to 400°F. Line 15×10-inch jelly-roll pan with heavy-duty foil. Coat both sides of each strip of bacon with brown sugar. Bake 18 to 20 minutes or until crispy. (Bacon should be turned over after 10 minutes).

S'MORE TREATS

MAKES 16 SERVINGS

2½ cups cocoa-flavored sweetened rice cereal

6 honey graham crackers, broken into ¼-inch pieces

3 tablespoons margarine

1½ teaspoons packed brown sugar

3½ cups mini marshmallows, divided

1 square (1 ounce) semisweet or milk chocolate, melted (optional)

1 Spray 9-inch square baking pan with nonstick cooking spray. Combine cereal and graham cracker pieces in large bowl.

2 Combine margarine and brown sugar in large microwavable bowl; microwave on HIGH 25 to 30 seconds or until margarine is melted. Add 2½ cups marshmallows; microwave on HIGH 1½ to 2 minutes, stirring after 1 minute or until marshmallows are melted and smooth.

3 Add marshmallow mixture to cereal mixture; stir to coat. Add remaining 1 cup marshmallows; stir until blended. Press evenly into prepared pan using waxed paper. Cool completely. Drizzle with chocolate, if desired. Cut into squares to serve.

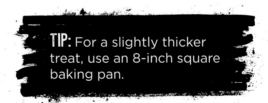

TIP: For a slightly thicker treat, use an 8-inch square baking pan.

DECADENT COCOA-OATMEAL COOKIES

MAKES 4 DOZEN COOKIES

½ cup (1 stick) unsalted butter, softened

½ cup granulated sugar

½ cup packed brown sugar

1 egg

½ teaspoon vanilla

¾ cup all-purpose flour

¼ cup unsweetened cocoa powder

½ teaspoon baking powder

1½ cups quick oats

1 cup milk chocolate chips

½ cup chopped macadamia nuts, toasted*

Toast chopped macadamia nuts in hot skillet over medium heat 3 minutes or until fragrant.

1 Preheat oven to 350°F. Line cookie sheets with parchment paper.

2 Beat butter in medium bowl with electric mixer at medium speed until light and fluffy. Add granulated sugar and brown sugar; beat until well blended. Add egg and vanilla; beat just until combined. Add flour, cocoa and baking powder; beat at low speed just until blended (dough will be sticky and stiff). Stir in oats, chocolate chips and nuts.

3 Shape dough into 1-inch balls. Place on prepared cookie sheets 2 inches apart. Slightly flatten each ball with back of spoon.

4 Bake 7 to 9 minutes or until firm around edges. Cool on cookie sheets 5 minutes. Remove to wire racks; cool completely. Store in airtight container.

PEANUT BUTTER S'MORES

MAKES 16 SANDWICH COOKIES

1½ cups all-purpose flour

½ teaspoon baking powder

½ teaspoon baking soda

¼ teaspoon salt

½ cup (1 stick) butter, softened

½ cup granulated sugar

½ cup packed brown sugar

½ cup creamy or chunky peanut butter

1 egg

1 teaspoon vanilla

½ cup chopped roasted peanuts (optional)

4 (1.55 ounces each) milk chocolate candy bars

16 large marshmallows

1 Preheat oven to 350°F.

2 Combine flour, baking powder, baking soda and salt in small bowl; set aside. Beat butter, granulated sugar and brown sugar in large bowl with electric mixer at medium speed until light and fluffy. Beat in peanut butter, egg and vanilla until well blended. Gradually beat in flour mixture at low speed until blended. Stir in peanuts, if desired.

3 Shape dough into 1-inch balls; place 2 inches apart on ungreased cookie sheets. Flatten dough with fork, forming criss-cross pattern. Bake about 14 minutes or until set and edges are lightly browned. Cool cookies 2 minutes on cookie sheets; transfer to wire cooling racks. Cool completely.

4 To assemble sandwiches, break each candy bar into 4 sections. Place 1 section of chocolate on flat side of 1 cookie. Place on microwavable plate; top with 1 marshmallow. Microwave on HIGH 10 to 12 seconds or until marshmallow is puffy. Immediately top with another cookie, flat side down. Press slightly on top cookie, spreading marshmallow to edges. Repeat with remaining cookies, chocolate and marshmallows, one at a time. Cool completely.

IRISH STOUT CARAMEL MILKSHAKE

MAKES 2 SERVINGS

Stout Caramel Sauce
(recipe follows)
1 pint (2 cups)
vanilla ice cream,
softened slightly
½ cup whole milk

1 Prepare Stout Caramel Sauce. Refrigerate until needed.

2 Combine ice cream, milk and ¼ cup Stout Caramel Sauce in blender. Blend on high 30 to 40 seconds or until smooth and frothy. Pour into 2 serving glasses and drizzle with additional Stout Caramel Sauce.

STOUT CARAMEL SAUCE

MAKES ABOUT 1⅓ CUPS SAUCE (ENOUGH FOR 4 BATCHES OF MILKSHAKES)

1 bottle (11.2 ounces)
Irish stout
1 cup sugar
1 cup whipping cream,
warmed until hot

Simmer stout in medium saucepan over medium heat until reduced to about ½ cup. Stir in sugar; continue cooking until mixture registers 275°F on candy thermometer. Remove from heat and carefully whisk in cream about ⅓ cup at a time. Let cool to room temperature. Transfer to airtight container and refrigerate, covered, at least 1 hour to thicken and cool completely.

ROCKY ROAD BUNDLES

MAKES 1 DOZEN TREATS

1 cup semisweet chocolate chips

½ cup creamy peanut butter

1 package (3 ounces) ramen noodles, any flavor,* broken into bite-size pieces

1 cup mini marshmallows

Discard seasoning packet.

1 Line baking sheet with waxed paper. Combine chocolate chips and peanut butter in large microwavable bowl. Microwave on MEDIUM (50%) 1 minute; stir. Repeat if necessary, stirring after 15-second intervals, until chocolate is melted and mixture is smooth.

2 Add noodles and marshmallows; mix well. Drop by tablespoonfuls onto prepared baking sheet; refrigerate 1 hour or until firm.

METRIC CONVERSION CHART

VOLUME MEASUREMENTS (dry)

$\frac{1}{8}$ teaspoon = 0.5 mL
$\frac{1}{4}$ teaspoon = 1 mL
$\frac{1}{2}$ teaspoon = 2 mL
$\frac{3}{4}$ teaspoon = 4 mL
1 teaspoon = 5 mL
1 tablespoon = 15 mL
2 tablespoons = 30 mL
$\frac{1}{4}$ cup = 60 mL
$\frac{1}{3}$ cup = 75 mL
$\frac{1}{2}$ cup = 125 mL
$\frac{2}{3}$ cup = 150 mL
$\frac{3}{4}$ cup = 175 mL
1 cup = 250 mL
2 cups = 1 pint = 500 mL
3 cups = 750 mL
4 cups = 1 quart = 1 L

VOLUME MEASUREMENTS (fluid)

1 fluid ounce (2 tablespoons) = 30 mL
4 fluid ounces ($\frac{1}{2}$ cup) = 125 mL
8 fluid ounces (1 cup) = 250 mL
12 fluid ounces (1$\frac{1}{2}$ cups) = 375 mL
16 fluid ounces (2 cups) = 500 mL

WEIGHTS (mass)

$\frac{1}{2}$ ounce = 15 g
1 ounce = 30 g
3 ounces = 90 g
4 ounces = 120 g
8 ounces = 225 g
10 ounces = 285 g
12 ounces = 360 g
16 ounces = 1 pound = 450 g

DIMENSIONS

$\frac{1}{16}$ inch = 2 mm
$\frac{1}{8}$ inch = 3 mm
$\frac{1}{4}$ inch = 6 mm
$\frac{1}{2}$ inch = 1.5 cm
$\frac{3}{4}$ inch = 2 cm
1 inch = 2.5 cm

OVEN TEMPERATURES

250°F = 120°C
275°F = 140°C
300°F = 150°C
325°F = 160°C
350°F = 180°C
375°F = 190°C
400°F = 200°C
425°F = 220°C
450°F = 230°C

BAKING PAN SIZES

Utensil	Size in Inches/Quarts	Metric Volume	Size in Centimeters
Baking or Cake Pan (square or rectangular)	8×8×2	2 L	20×20×5
	9×9×2	2.5 L	23×23×5
	12×8×2	3 L	30×20×5
	13×9×2	3.5 L	33×23×5
Loaf Pan	8×4×3	1.5 L	20×10×7
	9×5×3	2 L	23×13×7
Round Layer Cake Pan	8×1½	1.2 L	20×4
	9×1½	1.5 L	23×4
Pie Plate	8×1¼	750 mL	20×3
	9×1¼	1 L	23×3
Baking Dish or Casserole	1 quart	1 L	—
	1½ quart	1.5 L	—
	2 quart	2 L	—